Teaching
Four-Year-Olds:
A Personal Journey

by CAROL B. HILLMAN

PHI DELTA KAPPA
EDUCATIONAL FOUNDATION
Bloomington, Indiana

Cover design by Charmaine Shreve Dapena

Cover art, *My Sister Ava*, by Gina Mauro, a four-year-old in the author's class at The Nursery School, White Plains, New York.

Library of Congress Catalog Card Number 88-61775
ISBN 0-87367-799-4
Text copyright © 1988 by Carol B. Hillman
Photographs copyright © 1988 by Claire Yaffa

For the four-year-olds and their families,
who walk with me hand in hand.

TABLE OF CONTENTS

FOREWORD

I first met Carol Hillman when she enrolled in a seminar on educational administration taught by my husband and me at Bank Street College of Education in New York City. An on-going assignment for the seminar students was to keep a journal in which they recorded their feelings about their on-the-job experiences at school. Each week when the seminar met, the students would share what they had written in their journals.

The students' journal entries and the discussions that followed were an outpouring of anger and frustration — the rush to do more, to push down the curriculum into the lower grades, to use more and more workbooks at an earlier age, to test and test and test until the "weak spot" was found in each child, then to hurry and schedule remediation and test some more. The journal entries reflected the students' anguish over the agitation for teaching the "basics," the mounting demands for accountability, and the simplistic recipes for reform.

Then Carol would read from her journal, describing her everyday experiences as a nursery school teacher. The tense postures of the other students seemed to disappear; their facial expressions brightened; a calmness pervaded the seminar session. Carol talked about individual children in her class. Because she knew them so well, we, too, soon came to know them as individuals — their special talents, their favorite activities, their problems. She also talked about the class as a whole, about her teaching assistant, about her parents. We became caught up in the work she planned each day and the joy she seemed to derive from it. We heard about baking apple crisp and watching Monarch butterflies emerge from their chrysalids. We heard about making creatures with rose-colored playdough and feeding Italian parsely to a brown-and-white guinea pig. We gained new respect for the learning that comes from block play and became excited about the "Manhattan Project." We heard about the search for a green frog and the use of the autoharp to get the children's attention. We learned how little children can become engaged in BIG IDEAS as they make important decisions about their daily activities.

Carol's description of her work was without pretension, without pedagogical jargon. She told us what she did and how her life experiences had brought her to what she did. We knew we were hearing a professional. We knew that her classroom was a place where young children were learning about art, language, and number concepts; but more important, they were in a climate that fostered the dispositions to be friendly and helpful, to be curious, to take risks, to laugh, to love, and to learn.

Carol often refers to me as her mentor. While this is flattering, she really is reversing the roles, for it is she who has guided me, first in our seminar and now in this book, to see what early childhood education should be. What she has taught me will directly influence my work with others in my role as an elementary school principal, teacher educator, and workshop leader.

When Carol told me that Phi Delta Kappa was publishing her book, I was delighted not only for her but for the profession as a whole. The timing of the publication of this book is right on target. This is the time when formal programs for young children are being institutionalized nationwide. Almost all five-year-olds are now in kindergarten, and many kindergartens now offer full-day programs. Day-care centers and nursery schools under both public and private auspices are proliferating. With extended care programs, some young children are in "school" for as long as eleven hours a day. This is the time to ensure that we do right by those most vulnerable — the three-, four-, five-, and six-year-olds. Doing right means building the kind of learning communities for little children that Carol describes in this book.

It is my hope that this book will be read and discussed by teachers and administrators at staff meetings, by students in undergraduate and graduate courses in early childhood education, by parent groups at public and private nursery schools, and especially by the caregivers in day-care centers across the country.

I feel confident that each reader will sense, as I have, the wonder
and beauty — the possibility— of what good education for young
children can be.

JoAnn Shaheen, Principal
William O. Schaefer School
Tappan, New York
Adjunct Professor, Bank Street
College of Education, and
Associate Professor
State University of New York-New Paltz
August 1988

A PARENT'S PREFACE

My awareness of the world of a child began first with the birth of my two children and then as a photographer. As a mother and photographer, I have watched my children grow and learn to experience the world around them.

One of my son's first teachers was Carol Hillman. It was 15 years ago when she came to our home for the preschool visit she describes in this book. When she arrived, my son hid under his bed. Mrs. Hillman came into his room, laid down on the floor, and conversed with him as if this was nothing unusual.

She created a safe climate for him, and soon he crawled out from under his bed and enjoyed the world she wanted to share with him. A few years later, at another school, when my son didn't want to go on a class trip, he was locked in a closet until he stopped his hysterical crying.

In this book Carol Hillman writes about creating the kind of climate where children can explore the world and learn to feel good about themselves. She has dedicated her life to this purpose. It is my prayer and hope that all teachers of young children can create a climate where a child can crawl out from under his bed — but never be locked in a closet.

Claire Yaffa
August 1988

THE HIDDEN CURRICULUM

When someone asks me what I do, and I answer that I am a teacher of four-year-olds, I sometimes get the response: "What on earth can you teach them?" Many years ago I would have answered by describing some of the science projects or work with art materials I did with children. Now it is different: I feel more secure in my own position; I tell them what I really do. I teach children about the world they live in, about themselves and their peers. And I teach children about adults, trust, and love. I work with attitudes. I hope to inspire a love of learning. This is what I teach.

I want to know each child like I know the back of my hand. I want to recognize their voices from across the room so if I'm busy tying Sarah's shoes, I can answer without looking up. I want to know their wardrobes so I can recognize a new pair of shoe-laces or a new barrette when it is worn for the first time. I want to know what gives them pleasure and makes them smile. I want to know what really irritates them or makes them sad. I want to know what books they like to look at and what they like to eat. I want to know their favorite colors and their favorite stuffed animals. I want to know what scares them and what tickles their funny bone. I want to know the full range of their capabilities. I want to be able to read their eyes so I can tell if their day has not started well. I want to know a lot of things. And I want them to know that I know.

I want children to know themselves and feel good about what they know. I want children to recognize that there are areas in which they need to grow. I want children to learn to express themselves, but I accept the fact that some are not able to do that yet and are still fighting the world with their fists. I want children to come to terms with themselves, whatever those terms may be. I want to help each child accomplish these things through my caring.

I want children to respect each other for what they are. I want children to know that, although there are differences among them, these differences are what make each of them unique persons. I want them to know that people can change and that they all can help to make positive changes happen. I want them to know that we all have feelings and that each of us can feel hurt. And I want them to know how it feels to help another person.

I want children to know their teacher, to know her as a friend. I want children to know that adults are there to help them grow, to set limits, and to protect them. I want children to know that when they are sad or troubled, there is always a lap for them to climb on and receive comfort.

I want children to know that nursery school is now a big part of their world and that they are an important part of this world. I want children to know that this is where they are supposed to be and that Mommy and Daddy want them to be here. I want children to know that next year they will be in a different place and that they will be ready to leave here and move on to kinder-garten. This is what I teach. This is the hidden curriculum.

THE MASTER TEACHER

Because I have been teaching four-year-olds for many years, I am called a "Master Teacher." But longevity of the job is not what has earned me this title. Longevity can mean doing the same thing year after year. But there is little challenge in that or little satisfaction either. Rather, I am a Master Teacher because of the depth of experiences I have had over the years — experiences that have made me the person and teacher I am. Central to these experiences has been an attitude of wanting to grow, to continue learning. More than anything else, this attitude has sustained me in my work with young children.

There are, of course, many ways to grow. Some are pursued very deliberately; others are more subtle. Each, however, has its place in the scheme of things, and they all contribute to the kind of person and teacher one becomes. I deliberately get up at 5:30 a.m. each day and walk at a fast clip in order to keep myself in good physical shape and to keep my energy level high. Four years ago I deliberately made a decision to return to Bank Street College of Education in New York City, after an absence of 17 years, to seek a second advanced degree in supervision and administration. Returning to graduate school was intellectually stimulating; I was exposed to new books and ideas that had an immediate impact on my classroom techniques. And the people I met, who shared my professional interests, stimulated my thinking and helped me to assess where I was in relation to where I wanted to be. These were conscious and deliberate decisions that helped me to continue growing.

Less deliberate was a decision my former husband and I made many years ago to buy a farm in western Massachusetts. This brought a new and unexpected dimension into my life. I became enchanted with nature. I concentrated on growing things. I found delight in raising my own organic vegetables and small fruits. I went birding and spent hours observing the happenings at a beaver pond. I walked along an old dirt road in search of small red efts. I restored an abandoned apple orchard to its former productivity and beauty. I learned much about the ways of nature and continue to do so.

Each summer at my farm I grow milkweed in my garden to attract the Monarch butterfly. I collect caterpillars that emerge from the eggs that she lays and take them to school so the children can observe that miraculous metamorphosis. There, I take extended walks in quest of abandoned bird nests so the children can see how each species constructs its own special home. There, I dig ground pine and pipsissewa and gather British soldiers and star moss to make a natural habitat in an old glass fish bowl for the red efts that I find and take back to school. There, I can be assured of finding loads of lively crickets and earthworms from the compost, which I take back to my classroom as food for the toads. There, I gather bushels of McIntosh apple windfalls with which the children and I make our applesauce, baked apple slices, apple muffins, apple pancakes, and apple crisp. We even have apple snacks for our guinea pig, apples for the staff, and apples for all the children. There, I grow raspberries and make bright red jam that I cook in the sun, free from additives and preservatives. The children use this as a delicious topping for the homemade peanut butter we make by grinding the peanuts with freshly scrubbed cylinder blocks in a large wooden bowl.

There, I have learned to come to terms with a ribbon snake who likes to sun himself on the large flat rock by the side door. There, I have seen a resplendent red fox catching field mice after the meadow was mowed. There, I met a porcupine in the raspberry patch and asked aloud; "What are you doing here?" and soon found out. There, I have seen the matted grass in the orchard where the deer come to nibble the tender terminal buds of the apple trees before lying down to sleep. My encounters with animal life provide the material for stories I will later tell the children.

There, each summer I put my sleeping bag near the perennial garden and lie on my back to drink in the night sky. There, I sometimes rise early in the morning, before the sun is up, to tune my ears to the symphony of bird calls that greet each day. There I

4

take family and friends to share a special world from which I have learned so much and carry with me right into my classroom.

My first job after college was working in an art gallery in New York City, where I learned, among other things, how to hang an exhibition. This gave me a sense of space — a sense of how to use space to give emphasis and order to things. This is a skill that architects develop, and it is one that teachers can use in creating an attractive and orderly classroom environment.

I think like an architect as I decide how to display pictures in the classroom, dignifying each piece by mounting it on shiny colored paper obtained from the local printer. I think like an architect as I organize the space in my classroom. Blocks need shelves. Baskets of parquetry blocks, puzzles, and pegboards each need to stand apart and command their own sense of importance. These ordered arrangements are important. Visual effects are important. This is why the bookshelf in our library corner displays only a few titles at one time with their covers facing out.

Like an architect, I think about the difference it makes by grouping six children at one table rather than eight. I think about the ease of access to materials. I think about movement and the flow as children move through the morning involved in their various activities. It means placing a long piece of red Mystic tape on the floor directly in front of the block shelves to make a wide aisle where children are asked not to build in order that others have room to fetch the blocks they need for their building projects. During block play the unused blocks are put back on the shelves to make more floor space available to the four-year-old architects. It means being aware that block buildings are not too close to the children's cubbies. Cubbies are private places and should always be accessible to their owners. It means making sure that floor puzzles are not done in the passageways between our rooms and that the tow truck is not parked in the housekeeping corner, taking up valuable floor space.

Like an architect, I think about aesthetics, about establishing and maintaining a beautiful environment. Setting up a pleasing environment is easy. Maintaining that fresh and inviting look throughout the year demands far greater effort. With each day's art project, it means covering the tables with newspapers to keep them fresh, since paint or glue tends to find its way off the sheets of wallpaper or wood collages. It also means attending to our three easels and checking the paints each day. No muddy yellow is allowed to remain. Each morning the easels look like new.

As an architect, I am very aware of safety in the classroom, on the playground, and in our large-motor room. I make sure that the children wear hard hats when they build tall buildings or work near them. I make sure that floors are dried quickly when soapsuds or orange juice is spilled. I make sure that we have one-way traffic in the large-motor room on the tumbling mat and the balance beam. On the playground I watch out for children playing too near the swings.

Like an architect, I have learned many things about creating and maintaining an aesthetically pleasing environment in the classroom and about organizing space to facilitate traffic flow and ensure safety.

In the classroom I must be a scientist, too. I spend a lot of time watching what is going on because much is gained by observation. I spend more time listening and observing than talking. After our morning meeting in which everyone makes a plan for the day, I watch the children as they engage in their work. I want to be there as I am needed.

I often sit in a small orange chair in the corner of the block room, which is next to the housekeeping corner and not too far from the science area. From there, I can tie the bow at the back of a summer frock that has become a bridal gown or put our guinea pig on a child's lap and then put it back into its cage. From there, I can ask a few questions to expand the thinking of our builders: "How can you attach one building to another?" But basically I'm there to watch and to listen.

I keep my red leather notebook with me and spend some time writing anecdotal records. When the children ask what I'm doing, I tell them that I like to write things down about each one of them, that it's part of my work, like building is part of their work. Sometimes a question is asked and answered, but we soon go back to our jobs. I like sitting in my little orange chair because I'm learning. I can see that David has gained more self-control. Now he is talking about being angry instead of throwing blocks. He is trying hard to work things out. I like being there because I can see that Steven is still on the periphery of the group. He is still examining the equipment by himself and isn't ready to move in yet. I like being there in the presence of children.

I like to sit in my orange chair so I can think about what's to come. I like to listen to the children to find out what their interests are so that, together, we can build our curriculum. By listening and observing I can decide whether it's time to introduce pulleys and elevators for the block structures, or whether it is time to bring out the batteries and bulbs to make "The City" light up at night. Listening to and watching the children give me some ideas for the curriculum.

I like to be near the science corner because there is so much to learn from the animal life there. I want to be sure the guinea pig's cage is changed each day. Every day she needs fresh food and water with three drops of Vitamin C. I want to be sure someone sprays the red efts' terrarium to keep it moist. I want to make sure that the two small toads get their daily ration of mealworms. I like to be to be in the presence of children and animals to see their interactions.

I like to be near the housekeeping corner, too. I like to hear what is being served for breakfast, be it orange juice or pina coladas. I like to be nearby when the high heels and a gold lamé dress adorned with a fake fur stole go on, and one child turns to another to exclaim, "Hurry up, damn it; I'm late for the meeting!" As a scientist, I am there to listen and observe. I like being in the presence of children who also are listening, observing, and working things out.

As a teacher, I continue to learn in my roles as architect and scientist. But my ultimate role is as a caregiver, which to me means being a child advocate and a parent advocate. That is why I am here — to watch out for, to defend, and to nurture. In fulfilling this role, I first must win the trust of the parents. They must believe in me and the school. I want them to be teacher and school advocates. It must be a two-way street.

At parent orientation I tell the parents something about myself, my interests, and where and how I spend a good deal of my time. I share this information to open a dialogue and to begin the process of trust building. In this way I hope to ease the apprehension that many parents have when their child leaves home for the first time. Being a parent advocate carries its risks, too. Sometimes there is confrontation between two parents and subsequent anger, which I must mediate. It takes courage, but it is also part of the job.

As a caregiver I like the children to know I am there for them. I want them to know that each of them gets a turn at being "mail carrier," at delivering the week's paintings to each child's cubby, or at turning out the lights at rest time. They know it will happen because they see their names all written down in my red notebook. I watch to see that each child tries different activities. Sometimes I need to encourage a child to experience success by painting a maple leaf and making a print. I like to watch David at the workbench with hammer, nails, and brass jar lids and hear him shout, "Oh my God, a nail goes through metal!" I like it when a child looks up at me with that sense of wonder and says in a hushed tone, "I made pink!" I like it when Deborah rubs her tummy and says, "Yummy!" as she tastes the maple syrup that has been boiling down all week in the classroom. I like all children to feel good about what they do. With each success they are ready to try something new, to expand their horizons both socially and intellectually.

I am alert to times when things do not seem to be working out for a child. I watch when the corners of the mouth go down and the eyes fill with tears. When this happens there is a lap available, an arm to put around the shoulder, and a word of assurance that we can work things out together. I am alert to behaviors that indicate growth in social sensitivity, when a child says, "Stop, you are not allowed to push in front of John!" or "No, you may not take blocks from Elisabeth's building!"

As a Master Teacher, I continue to learn as an architect, a scientist, a caregiver, and a child and parent advocate. There is great satisfaction in all of this learning.

THE END OF SUMMER

It is the end of August. I am sitting at the kitchen table at my farm in western Massachusetts gazing beyond the explosion of color provided by the faithful phlox to the Quabbin Reservoir. There is something soothing about the ever-changing but ever-present view before me. Westchester County (and my work at The Nursery School) is only three hours away, but the psychological distance makes it seem far greater.

Separations, endings, and beginnings are very much a part of our lives; and so it is with teaching. As I think ahead to our first staff meeting, I tell myself how truly grateful I am for the inner strength that comes from being close to the earth. At the same time, I am truly grateful that I am going back to work, where what I do counts in the lives of four-year-olds and their parents.

Last week a small red eft ambled lazily over the fieldstone path toward my back door. Seeing it reminded me that "It's that time of year again." Gathering red efts and making them a beautiful woodsy environment with mosses, ground pine, and pipsissewa is one of my end-of-summer rituals. It is part of the transition back to school. I delight in walking along the dirt road after a rain to see how many red efts I can find. The only equipment needed is a small plastic bag — and a sharp eye.

I have been collecting Monarch caterpillars and bringing them to my classroom for many years. I want the children to observe this miracle of nature — the metamorphosis of caterpillar to chrysallis to butterfly. The Monarch lays her eggs only on milkweed, the sole food supply of the caterpillar. Some years ago it dawned on me that if I grew milkweed in my own garden, I could save myself a lot of time searching for these creatures. This has been a banner year. I found at least 20 in the garden, many just sitting on top of the milkweed leaves, and half a dozen more in

9

the adjacent meadow. The present excitement for me is finding these beauties. The future excitement is back at school where the children will see them pass through the metamorphosis stages to become beautiful butterflies. This, too, is part of the transition back to school.

Early this summer I caught a handsome green frog with golden eyes. My friend, Robert, built a sturdy wood-framed wire cage for him. I constructed a grand pond from an old blue enameled loaf pan surrounded with rocks and layers of moss and pine needles. He was such fun, such a sportive frog. When my grandson Lawrence came to visit, we set up a small plastic swimming pool and froggie went swimming with him. I wanted to keep him to take back to school in the fall. But I let froggie go. I could not deny him the freedom of his summer. So, there is work to be done. I am on the lookout for one green frog and one American toad!

The most important thing about the end of the summer is to feel positive about the months behind as well as the months ahead. As you think about the months ahead when you return to your classroom of four-year-olds, ask yourself these questions:

1. Did you have a plan for learning something new this summer that would make a difference in your teaching?
2. Have you considered keeping a journal of your experiences and your thoughts?
3. Have your experiences this summer given you some new ideas for the classroom?
4. Have you collected any new materials for the classroom?
5. Have you thought about bringing in some new animals for your science program?
6. Did you set aside some time for personal reading?
7. Were you able to visit with family and friends in a leisurely fashion?
8. Have you stayed in contact with other staff members?
9. Do you feel enriched by your vacation in ways that you can take back to the classroom?
10. Are you looking forward to teaching again?

HOME VISITS

I like meeting children for the first time on their own turf. Making a home visit allows me to enter the child's world. It says that I am interested in the whole child, which includes every family member. It says that I recognize the vital importance of the home atmosphere in the child's life. The classroom is, after all, only part of a child's world.

I spend about 30 minutes on a home visit. Usually the parents will ask me to sit down in the living room for a little talk. However, long ago I decided that a formal chat is not the best way to begin. Instead, I say, "Bryan, how about showing me your room?" And I go scampering up the stairs with Bryan in the lead.

I want to see his toys and let him tell me which one he likes to play with the most. I look at his books and perhaps read him a story. I may sit on the floor with him and watch him do a butterfly puzzle, or I may challenge him to a game of "Go Fish" if he enjoys playing cards. I look at the photographs in his room and let him tell about his pals at day camp. I hold and pat his favorite teddy bear and try to remember its name. I try to spot any toys or books that we also have in the classroom to help him make connections at the beginning of the school year. I invite him to bring his much-loved teddy bear or a favorite record or tape to play at school. I want Bryan to know that there are many similarities between our worlds and that the toys that he cherishes can also come to school.

I look at his play equipment outside and watch him perform his latest climbing feat. I admire the garden that he has planted and taste a cherry tomato he picked for me. I watch him ride his bicycle with training wheels, and we check out the small stream that runs alongside his house. I want to sense how he spends his time and what gives him the greatest pleasure.

I want to see his baby brother asleep in his crib. I want to see his big sister's room, even though she is not at home this morning, having already started school. I want to meet all members of the household, for they, too, are a big part of his life.

I want to meet the family dog or cat and hold the soft, furry rabbit that lives in a tall wooden cage in the back yard. I want to see his fish tank and talk about the different species and how he cares for them. I want Bryan to show me what is important in his life.

As Bryan's teacher, I come to his home so I can understand his world and begin to lay the groundwork for a year of learning. I come so that Bryan knows who I am and what I look like. I come so that when Bryan arrives at school the first day, he will be warmly greeted by a familiar face and a familiar voice.

A week ago I was in line to have my car washed and noticed a familiar face in the car behind me. I remembered Mrs. Yaffa and asked how Robbie was. She told me that he was doing beautifully and was looking at colleges for next fall. The next thing she said was: "Do you remember your home visit when you crawled under the bed to talk to Robbie because he was so shy?"

The most important thing about home visits is meeting children for the first time on their own turf — even if it means crawling under the bed to meet them.

There is much that can be learned from a home visit. Some questions to ask yourself are:

1. Are there other children or adults, other than the parents, in the household?
2. Was there a sense of order about the home and the child's room?
3. Does the child share a room, and if so, with whom?
4. Did the parent allow the child to take you to his room by himself?
5. Are the child's toys age-appropriate?
6. Did you talk to the child about his favorite toy, meet his pet, or look at a favorite book with him?
7. What did you observe about the quality of the relationship between parents and child?
8. Did you leave enough time between home visits to start your anecdotal records on the child?

SETTING UP THE CLASSROOM

I am greatly affected by my surroundings, and I assume that young children are, too. One of the joys of teaching is setting up the classroom to make it a special place for the children. What you choose to have in your room and how you arrange it creates the learning environment. As a teacher, you both design and set the stage.

I am fortunate at the school in which I work because I am given many choices. I can decide about the materials I use. I can decide about the color of the walls or the need for new shelves. I appreciate having the right to make those decisions.

My classroom is really two rooms separated by an accordion door. I didn't choose this arrangement, but it works because there is a clear line of demarcation creating a different atmosphere in each space. Our rooms are painted a cheerful pastel yellow accented with a pastel orange. As you enter the room, the first impression is one of light. The entire eastern exposure is glass, allowing the sun to stream in all morning, warming our bodies and raising our spirits. We use those expansive windows to make our own "stained glass" windows with waxed paper and brightly colored cellophane. Just three weeks ago Jennifer noticed that when the shade was pulled down a bit, you could see a silhouette of a house sparrow sitting on a vine growing up the outside wall. The big windows bring the world of nature outside into our classroom.

I like a classroom to be not only bright and cheerful but to have a sense of definition so that, when the children come in, they will know what goes on in each area of the room. This spatial definition reminds the children that the world has a sense of order and that school has it, too.

13

One element of order is a cubby for each child — a special private place that belongs to each child every day he comes to school. John's name is there, printed in red letters on a bright yellow paper circle. In the top section of his cubby, there is a floral design plastic bag to hold his extra clothing. Below are two hooks to hang a jacket, a backpack, or whatever he wants. Below that is another space for John's rest mat. Cubbies serve many purposes, such as safeguarding a toy when, at the moment, sharing it with classmates is out of the question. I have also seen a cubby used as a source of comfort, much like the way a young child fingers the satin binding of a favorite blanket. I have seen a child crawl into his cubby, thumb in mouth and head cast down, not wanting to be part of the group and keeping his distance from the world. It is important to have your own place, especially when you are only four.

Each of our two rooms is 15 by 25 feet. In the first room are three tables; two are pushed together to seat eight and the other table seats six. On our big table I usually lay out materials for the art project of the day. When the children come bounding into the room and see the materials, they pepper me with questions: "What are we doing with those big pieces of white chalk and styrofoam and the black paper?" or "What are those pieces of evergreen for?" Such questions are more an indication of their enthusiasm to undertake a new project than they are a quest for answers.

To the left of the big table is a shelf for art supplies, including construction paper and magic markers. There are four cigar boxes painted fire-engine red, each holding two small juice containers for paint. There is a white rectangular tray lined in bright blue paper for eight pairs of Crayola plastic scissors. Another white tray lined with blue holds four jars of Elmer's glue and craft sticks. A third tray holds the cookie cutters and one miniature muffin pan for the playdough. There are old wooden rolling pins, a white plastic-covered container filled with rose-colored playdough, and a stack of pressed-wood rectangles that serve as artist palettes.

A built-in easel, large enough for three children to paint at one time, stretches across part of the north wall. Above it is mounted a thin strip of wood with hooks for displaying paintings only moments after the artist has announced they are finished. Nearby is our sink with a supply cabinet over it. Gallon jugs of paint sit on top of the cabinet. Directly across from the real sink are the "pretend" sink and stove, where young chefs cook up and serve strawberry pizza or marshmallow cake. Soap flakes and water along with basters, beaters, whisks, funnels, pumps, and pitchers are all used for a variety of experiences that can take place in this area.

Another section of the first room is our library corner. It is carpeted and has big floppy blue pillows to curl up on and chairs to sit on. Our record player is in the library corner, where, at any given moment, one might hear Raffi's "Down by the Bay" being played to tickle a child's fancy. If a child is tired, he is free to take his rest mat to the library corner or to sit on a teacher's lap and listen to a story.

This is our quieter room where a child can do puzzles or table games at the small table. It is the room where we put out the playdough on the day the children come back after a school vacation, because it is a quiet activity and helps the children to settle back gradually into classroom routines. It is the room in which to sit and watch a small red eft crawl up the sides of its own basket, a room to thumb quietly through a favorite book or to discover a new one. It is a room to work on the butterfly matching game at your own pace or just to have a quiet conversation with your teacher.

The atmosphere I want to create in our first room is a low-keyed place of quiet stimulation. By designing and then setting up the classroom space, I am able to create this atmosphere.

Our other room is quite different. It has the same expanse of windows and the same number of cubbies, but three-quarters of the south wall is lined with shelves to hold the blocks and other wooden accessories. The two other areas in this room are the housekeeping corner and the science corner, which are divided by a shelf.

We recently made some changes in this room. One suggestion came from Jack, one of our four-year-olds. He suggested moving the rocking chair from the library corner in the other room, where it had been forever, into the science corner. With the rocking chair in the science corner, said Jack, a person who wanted to hold our guinea pig could rock it as well. I think Jack had a great idea. The other suggestion came from a visiting teacher from the Bank Street College of Education in New York City, who conducted

15

two sessions with the staff on blockbuilding. She pointed out that if I moved the shelf divider separating the housekeeping and block-building areas, then the housekeeping activities would not spill over into the blockbuilding area. This seems to have worked well, too. By being open to change, which in this case was simply moving the divider, I was able to improve the working space for the blockbuilding projects.

Part of setting up the classroom is being a collector, and being a collector requires ample space to store what you have collected. My solution was adding two new sets of shelves for five-gallon ice cream containers, which I have covered with orange contact paper. I have 30 such containers all filled to the brim with sea shells, sweet gum pods, birds' nests, pine cones, doll furniture, fabric, hand puppets, and many, many more things. I also have corrugated rectangular bins, which are painted a pastel yellow. These are filled with paper towel cylinders, toilet tissue rolls, egg cartons, extra juice cans, boxes of every description, and much more. All the storage containers are labeled by gluing a piece of their contents on the outside of the container. This makes it easy for me to find things when I need them.

Collecting things is part of the nursery school teacher's job, but it helps to have a network of collectors to assist you. I have one friend who saves cardboard, another who squirrels away juice cans, and a son-in-law who provides me with bags of film cannisters for the whole school. I like being a collector. There is a certain satisfaction in putting things to use that would otherwise be cast aside.

The noise level in the block area is high because of the physical activity there. And sometimes there is controversy, too. Charles wants to build the bridge using square blocks, but Michele wants to use the unit blocks. There is lots of talking, occasional whining, and sometimes grabbing. Now and then a building comes crashing down. But mostly there is a sense of purpose as the children concentrate on the serious work of planning and constructing. The blockbuilding area is where the action is.

In the housekeeping corner there are spirited voices, too. Mommies and daddies and crying babies and bossy older brothers and sisters are going to the hospital, or cooking supper for the family, or just carrying on a conversation. Just the other day Lauren said to Tony, "When I marry you, you'll have to stop sucking your thumb."

16

Part of the joy of teaching is setting up the classroom, making it a beautiful environment. You both design and set the stage. You create the climate where children learn through play. The most important thing about setting up the classroom is creating a physical and emotional climate that allows for optimal learning.

Some important questions to ask yourself are:

1. Does each child have his own special space?
2. Have you created a visually pleasing environment?
3. Are the work areas clearly defined to give a sense of order in the room?
4. Are the newspapers covering the easels fresh each day?
5. Are the pictures on your walls dog-eared and faded?
6. Are the dress-up clothes in the housekeeping corner washed and ironed occasionally?
7. Have you devised a good system for storing and marking materials used in the classroom?
8. Is all the equipment you use in good repair?
9. Have you created a safe environment for your children?

CREATING A SAFE AND SECURE ENVIRONMENT

When the children burst into my classroom, their faces awash with joy and anticipation and talking a mile a minute, it flashes across my mind how precious childhood is. It gives me great pause when I consider the trust these parents have placed in my hands. I take very seriously the responsibility of caring for other people's children. Sometimes it frightens me.

Safety must be considered first and foremost in every activity we do throughout the school day. The children help me to keep our room a safe place, but what happens in the classroom is primarily my responsibility. Very early it becomes apparent to the children that I don't want anyone hurt, that I watch out for each of them. No child is allowed to leave the classroom without the teacher knowing his whereabouts. This is a form of caring; it is also a form of safety. No child is allowed to hit, push, or bite another child. This, too, is a form of caring, a form of safety. No child is allowed to use harsh or teasing words that make another person feel unhappy. That is an important form of caring and safety also. Physical and emotional safety go hand in hand in creating a secure environment.

As a teacher, I set the standards for the children. As a teacher, I model what I expect of them. These expectations permeate the classroom atmosphere and become the goals we strive to achieve. These classroom expectations are very real and very necessary components of our life at school.

Safety begins with respect, and I make the first move. I respect each child. I strive to have each child respect me. I teach and support every child's effort to respect his classmates. It takes all kinds of doing to earn this respect, but that is where safety must begin.

Children who have not yet learned to take turns may strike out at other children. Safety is letting the children know that words, not fists, are the way we convey our thoughts to other people. Sometimes I have to ask a child to reflect on his actions and talk it over with me.

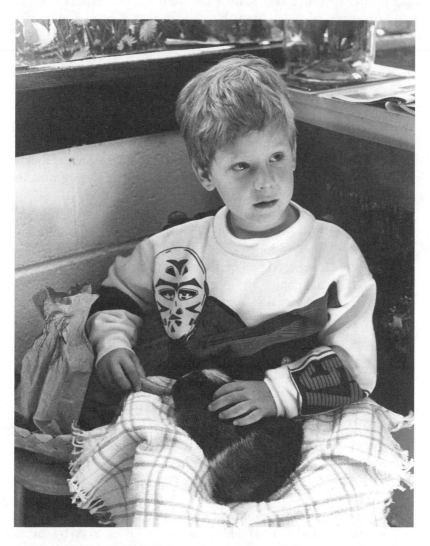

Stroking "Little Nose," the guinea pig, provides a quiet diversion from the bustling activity of the day

Safety is seeing that toys can be shared and that people can take turns. Safety is setting up rules: only two people may work at the workbench at a time; woodworkers must wear goggles. Safety is insisting that there is no running in the classroom. Safety is making it clear that blocks are not to be walked on because they can slide across the floor and cause one to fall. Safety is seeing that only three people work with soapsuds at a time and that newspaper is spread on the floor before they start. Safety is mopping up a sea of suds when the yellow plastic bowl spills over onto the floor.

Safety involves a lot of cleaning up and picking up — often on a moment's notice and no matter whatever else is going on. It means picking up parquetry blocks, puzzle pieces, tinker toys, and pieces from table games from the floor and putting them in their proper places. It means putting the plastic dishes back on the shelf and hanging up the evening gowns in the housekeeping corner. Safety means wearing hard hats when building with blocks. Safety means not climbing on the block shelf or sitting on the workbench.

Safety is showing children how to walk with the scissors pointing down and how to carry a chair so the legs don't hit another child or knock down a block construction. Safety is putting a cork on the tip of an exposed nail on the rocket ship made at the workbench. Safety is keeping the paring knife and the matches on a high shelf out of a child's reach.

Safety involves maintenance, too. When the tail of a wooden airplane is shattered, it is removed from the top of the block shelf until it is repaired. When a plastic cup is broken, it is glued back together. If the edge of a wooden block is splintered, it is sanded down.

Safety is setting up ground rules wherever the children are — in the classroom or on the playground. On the playground with its large open spaces, spirits can run high. There are spots that get muddy when the ground begins to thaw, and puddles appear after a heavy downpour. There is heavy metal climbing equipment, which must be moved only by the teachers. There is a slide where one-way traffic is mandatory. There are woods surrounding our playground where children are not allowed to go by themselves. Ground rules are needed for all of these potential safety hazards.

Children like rough and tumble games, running and rolling on the ground, but it can get out of hand. Sometimes I have to say, "If Andrew is getting too rough, you need to say, 'Stop, I don't want to play anymore'." Or I say, "Stop. You are being too rough; I'm afraid someone is going to get hurt." Rules have to be repeated for both the classroom and the playground. As the teacher, I need to reinforce these ground rules time and time again.

Sometimes a child will taunt or tease another child in a sing-song manner, and then other children will pick up the refrain. I try to nip this behavior in the bud by doing an exaggerated imitation of the sing-song teasing. Hearing this mocking tone from their teacher, the class responds with giggles. They soon get the point. Safeguarding young children's feelings is a full-time job in the nursery school. It is part of the job of making school a secure place.

I have moments when I feel overwhelmed with my responsibility of caring for other people's children. I have many more moments when I delight in just being with children and creating a safe and secure environment for them. The most important thing about creating a safe environment is constant awareness and vigilance.

Some important questions to ask yourself are:

1. Do you consider the safety factors related to every activity you undertake in the classroom or on the playground?
2. Have you repeatedly expressed your concern about safety directly to the children?
3. Have you asked the children to share the responsibility of keeping the classroom a safe place for them?
4. How will you let the children know ahead of time that they will be removed from an activity if they are having difficulty controlling their behavior?
5. Is your room equipped with cleaning supplies such as a mop, broom, dustpan, sponges, and a pile of newspapers?
6. Are you consistent about keeping paring knives, matches, and potentially harmful liquids out of the reach of children?
7. Have you developed a system for patrolling the playground and being alert to conditions affecting the safety of the children?
8. Are you aware when a child is unusually quiet?
9. Do you role model the type of behavior you expect from the children?

PARENT ORIENTATION

My memories of attending Parents' Night for my own children are not particularly pleasant. I usually left wondering whether my child was receiving the individual attention that I thought was needed. The message for parents seemed to be, "Don't call us, we'll call you." As parents we were seldom asked to participate in any way beyond cooking for a bake sale or working on a fund-raising project. I wondered then if it had to be that way. Now, I know it does not have to be that way.

Parent orientation in my school is quite different from what I experienced as a parent. Our classroom doors are always open. We welcome parents, grandparents, and especially the children's siblings. Children are proud to share their school world with those who are close to them. I think young children get a message when there is free-flowing communication between school and home. They seem to sense the spirit of cooperation at work in their be-half. They feel good that there is a support system of both teachers and parents close at hand.

Sending something to school is a good way of communicating. A shared home activity such as making homemade cranberry bread or gathering a bag of McIntosh apples from a "pick your own" orchard is particularly nice. One year a grey-and-white Dutch Belted rabbit became a permanent resident in our classroom. Another year a hermit crab took up residence in our science cor-ner. Each was an exciting event for the class, the teachers, the parents, and most of all for the giving child. There is something quite special about the smile and inward joy of a young giver.

There are other ways of communicating that should become routine. I like to write a note or pick up the telephone to ask a parent if we could have a few minutes to talk in the hall on a carpool day. The message I want to convey is that I am available. I can be called at home. I don't consider this an imposition or an intrusion in my life. It is part of my life.

In a course on family, child, and teacher interaction I recently took at Bank Street College of Education, one of the requirements was to write an autobiography to be shared with our classmates. We asked our instructor, an erudite and gentle woman, to do the same. She agreed to do so at the last class session. I was moved by the way she shared so much about herself and vowed that I would begin the year by sharing some things about my life with my pupil's parents. As I thought about it over the summer, I realized that if I took the lead and set the tone for sharing, similar sharing by my parents could be forthcoming.

I decided not to talk about where I came from but rather about what captivates my interest and heart now. I felt good about telling the parents how I restored an abandoned apple orchard, using as few chemicals as possible. I felt good about sharing with them my joy in working the earth and being with family and friends on the farm. I will feel even better if my openness about sharing will prompt even one parent to share with me.

The most important thing about parent orientation is creating an atmosphere that invites open, honest communication between parents and the teacher. Some things to think about when meeting parents are:

1. Are name tags, adult-size chairs, and a convenient coat rack available?
2. Have you provided parents with emergency cards so that you can reach them during the day if necessary?
3. Have you made it clear that you would like the meeting to be mutual sharing and not a one-way conversation?
4. Have you scheduled your time so that you can be at school well in advance of the announced meeting time in order to talk informally with any early arrivals?
5. Have you planned your presentation to cover both classroom routines and a philosophical overview of the year's program?
6. Will you emphasize the importance of close cooperation between teacher and parents in the child's behalf?
7. Will you make known your own availability including your home telephone number?

8. Will you take the lead in discussing something about yourself in order to give parents some insights about you as a person?
9. Are you planning to serve refreshments after the meeting?
10. Have you by word and deed conveyed the message that you are both a child advocate and a parent advocate?

THE FIRST FEW DAYS OF SCHOOL

The beginning of school should be as easy as possible for all concerned. We do several things to "ease" the children into a new world and new routines. Each of our first two days is only an hour long, and only half of the class comes at a time. On the third and fourth days we meet for two hours with the full class. Then on the fifth day, all the children attend the full morning session of two hours and 45 minutes. It is a gentle beginning in which the children gradually become accustomed to their new environment.

On these first days we try to do everything in small groups. Being in a small group helps to make one feel big. The children get to know each other when we sit together at one table for juice and crackers. In a small group it doesn't take too long for everyone to have a turn holding the brown-and-white guinea pig, to feed her Italian parsley, and to brush her with a small red-handled baby brush. In a small group we can get to know each other's names and practice using them. In a small group we can explore the room, locating where the long paintbrushes are kept and where the yellow smocks are hung. In a small group we can listen to a story and take turns sitting close to the teacher. A small group is a lot like being in a family, which is really what we are trying to be.

I ask that the parents stay close by those first few days. It is an hour or two out of their schedule, but it can mean so much for their child. At Parent Orientation I say to the parents, "I want you in the classroom, to be there for your child." I ask each parent to find a spot to sit down so they will be at the child's level and to bring a book to read or some handwork to do. With Mom or Dad nearby, the children can go to them if they need comforting or reassurance. Then, at juice and cracker time, I ask the parents to leave and have their coffee or tea across the hall. It seems a logical time for that first separation, and it is easier for the children if the parents move out as a group. It's the first goodbye of nursery school. Mom and Dad are only 15 steps away, but it is the first goodbye.

I explain to parents that the first separation can be upsetting to some children. Some children require more time than others, and parents should not feel any embarrassment if their child needs a little longer to adjust to the separation. Some children can say goodbye more easily than the parents. Sometimes I have to convince a parent that it's really time to go. Whatever the case, I take the parents and child where they are and help them work through the situation.

Life is a series of separations. We can accept the tears and acknowledge that Elaine is sad, but we reassure her that Mommy or Daddy will return to meet her on the playground. In the meantime, she knows there are other adults who will care for her in their absence, and that she will be able to manage without them for a while.

During the first few days of school, the teacher must make special efforts to be both a child and parent advocate. Small groups help to create a family atmosphere and provide a setting that is comfortable for the children and their parents.

The most important things to remember about the first few days of school are to respect the children and to create a place that is comfortable for them and for their parents.

Some important questions to ask yourself are:

1. Did you lay the groundwork for the opening days of school at your parent orientation? Have you written out the standard routines to give parents at the orientation?
2. Is it possible to set up a schedule for the opening days of school so that only half the children come at one time for an hour or so?
3. Will you invite parents to be part of the beginning and to stay in the classroom with their children?
4. Have you arranged for refreshments for parents in another room in the building?
5. Have you limited the number of toys on display those first few days so the children will not be overstimulated with all the new things to play with?

The first few days of school are a gentle beginning in which children gradually become accustomed to their new environment.

6. Can you structure your abbreviated beginning days so that the children and parents get a sense of what a regular day is like?
7. Will you have all your preparations done for the day so that you can devote your full attention to the children when they arrive?
8. Will you remember that children will react differently as they enter a new environment, with different expectations, unfamiliar classmates, and a new teacher? How will you respond to these different reactions?
9. In what ways will you show that you appreciate and respect each child?

THE TEACHER OF YOUNG CHILDREN

I think a good teacher of young children should try to be all-seeing rather than all-knowing, a good listener rather than a constant talker. The emphasis should be on observation and interpretation rather than relying on past experience for solving every problem that arises.

I think a good teacher of young children should look at the children's interests in planning the curriculum rather than relying on last year's lesson plans. The emphasis should be on the expressed needs of each child rather than on preconceived notions of what is good for young children in general.

There are many things good teachers of young children need to be. The first is a spirit of willingness. They need to be willing to look at the world with a fresh approach, willing to run their finger over the ridges of a scallop shell and talk about the way it feels. They need to be willing to sing a favorite song like "Pitter Patter" over and over again. They need to be willing to comfort a child whose mommy is late for an appointment and cannot stay to watch him complete the big floor puzzle of the farm. They need to be willing to praise and to express pleasure in a child's rocket ship, which he designed with the colored wooden shapes and small brass nails. They need to be willing to show physical affection — a hug, a pat on the head, an arm around a shoulder — and to know that this is all right to do.

Good teachers of young children should have a sense of fun — making up silly rhymes, singing some silly songs, or listening to silly "knock-knock" jokes that tickle a four-year-old's funny bone.

A teacher of young children needs to be able to say, "No, it's too late to start a painting today. You can be first to paint tomorrow." A teacher of young children needs to be able to say, "Stop! I will not allow you to push Julia. She may get hurt, and I want

28

to take good care of everyone in the class." A teacher of young children needs to let it be known that she believes in what she says, even at the risk of confrontation.

A good teacher of young children needs to take great pleasure in setting up a classroom that allows children to explore, to question, to work alone, in a group, or with an adult. A good teacher of young children needs to be willing to be the same kind of learner that she expects each child in her class to be.

The most important thing about being a teacher of young children is a willingness to learn about a child by being with a child and responding to a child.

Some important questions to ask yourself are:

1. How do you show children that you value listening to them?
2. As you listen to children's conversations, are you discovering ideas that can be incorporated into the curriculum?
3. Can you engage in the repetitive activities that young children love without becoming bored?
4. Can you still get excited with the children about the first snowfall, the magic of a single flake on a child's nose?
5. Do you find more things to praise than to fault?
6. Because of recent publicity about child molestation in a day-care center in California, do you think twice before hugging a child?
7. Is it beneath your dignity to wear a flowered hat if a child places it on your head?
8. Do you admit to making mistakes? Do you take action to rectify them?
9. Do you do what has to be done knowing full well that there are times you may make a child angry?
10. How will you make your classroom a stimulating learning environment?

FINDING THE POSITIVES IN CHILDREN

I like to dwell on positives in working with children. Accentuating the positive helps children stay in forward gear. It's better to focus on the good than to call attention to the not so good. It's better to praise than to damn. Being positive promotes harmony and lessens discord. However, being positive is not always easy.

Jim is back for his second year in the four-year-olds class. It was a difficult decision for his parents, who are well-educated people. They waited until late May to make the decision.

Jim is a featherweight, only about 28 pounds with his overalls and jacket on. He looks as if a slight wind might blow him away, but looks can be deceiving. He is a powerhouse of energy and pursues ideas with single-minded determination. Jim entered my classroom ready to do battle, ready to test me and to resist authority. My first clue about Jim's behavior came early when he ignored the cleanup time warning and continued his project of nailing brightly colored shapes onto a painted green acoustical tile — a well-conceived design. I noted it in my daily anecdotal record.

The next day as I was tagging the wing of a Monarch butterfly before releasing it for its migration south, Jim came and stood next to me in front of the butterfly cage. He asked if he could hold a butterfly. I told him, "Yes, just give me a minute to finish this." In a flash I saw those tiny hands dart past me and grab another Monarch that was resting on the netting covering the cage. He squeezed it hard.

The next day Jim's mother was on the playground with her younger child in tow. She shared with me her ambivalent feelings about keeping Jim a second year in nursery school. Now she wasn't so sure that she and her husband had made the right decision. She recently had heard that the kindergarten where Jim had been scheduled to go was quite unstructured, and perhaps he could have done well in such an environment. I wondered how much of this attitude was getting through to her very perceptive son.

Each day another incident or two with Jim occurred. He hit another child with a metal "S" hook that is attached to our wooden tug boat. He knocked down another child's block building with deliberate kicks. He pushed his way into the cleanup line. He took a baster filled with soap suds and squirted it on Bert's face and shirt. These far from positive behaviors seemed to be Jim's style.

A second lengthy conversation with Jim's mother revealed that she was aware that things were not running as smoothly as she had hoped. Jim had reported at home that because he wouldn't help with cleanup, he wasn't allowed to have a snack. While this was not the case, it was his way of telling his mother that something was awry. I took the opportunity to tell her that I thought it was important for Jim to have another year in nursery school in order to have more time to develop social relationships with his peers and his teacher before he jumped into the "big time" of kindergarten.

I shared with her some of the things that were happening, and she in turn opened up about difficulties at home. She shared her concerns about his stubbornness, his resistance to authority, and even lying. Clearly, she was frustrated over what to do about his behavior.

I suggested that she sit down with her husband and talk about priorities for Jim. I sensed that Jim and his mother were in a power struggle and something had to break that lock. Without some overhauling, there would be no shifting gears, no forward motion. I recommended that she try to ease the pressure so Jim could feel some measure of personal control. I also asked her to tell Jim that we had talked, emphasizing the importance of candor among a parent, teacher, and child. She complied.

Things are moving now. We are indeed in first gear. Each limit has been clearly redefined. Jim knows the rules of the game and knows they must be kept.

Jim is both bright and musically talented. I decided I would appeal to those two attributes in order to give him a feeling of importance in the class. He brought a book to school, the story of "The Three Little Pigs." As I was reading it to the class, the word "fiddle" appeared in the text and I asked Jim if he knew another word for it. He shot back, "violin." I knew he played the violin, so I asked if he would like to bring it to school and play for us. He beamed as he said he would.

His mom knows that he has had two good days. It is important that she knows. It's a beginning. We are starting to dwell on positives. It's easier to accentuate the good. It's better to praise. It's more pleasant to work in harmony. We are starting to roll, and I am excited.

The most important thing about using the positives is that they improve the chances of helping a child grow.

Some important questions to ask yourself are:

1. Are you clear and consistent about classroom expectations?
2. How would you involve other children in helping a child with difficulties?
3. Do you have a system for keeping anecdotal records to use when discussing a child's behavior with parents?
4. Do you have a plan to help parents work toward specific goals with their child?
5. What methods will you use to identify special interests or talents a child may have?
6. How will you confront the child who is disrupting the classroom?
7. Are you alert to opportunities to give praise often?
8. In what ways can positive reinforcement be used in order to lessen the need for disciplining?

TIME TO EVALUATE

We are a month into the school year. Eight more months of opportunity lie ahead, but it's already time to sit down and evaluate where we are. Having my new assistant, Ann, in the classroom is a good way of keeping me on my toes. As the role model, I feel a special responsibility to do the very best I can in the classroom. It isn't easy to keep up high standards consistently, but no one ever said teaching was going to be easy.

Evaluation can occur in many settings. I like to sit down regularly with my assistant over lunch or a cup of coffee and talk openly. When any two people work together, there are small things that one would like to see changed. The hardest part can be in the telling, but it doesn't have to be that way. So much has to do with the atmosphere created, with the way one communicates — the tone of voice, the body language, the eye contact. It's the blending of these elements that makes the telling easier.

My assistant, Ann, and I have talked often during these first four weeks, either before school in the morning as we are setting up the room or after carpool when the children have gone. My main thrust has been to praise her for her good work: her modulated voice when she speaks to the children, her ability to see where she is needed, and the unobtrusive way she goes about doing what has to be done. I have offered her suggestions when the need arises: "Be down at the child's level as much as possible. Write their names in the left hand corner of their paintings. Keep the art table always looking fresh and inviting." All this contributes to our working as a team, with the same goals in mind.

People need to be told that they are good at their job and are appreciated. A part of my job in evaluation is to tell Ann that and to mean it. And I do! I also invite her to question my actions. And she does! Communication must never be a one-way street.

Once we finish talking about ourselves, we go on to talk about the children, discuss changes we have observed and the reasons for those changes. Listening is where it all begins. The next step is acting on what one has heard.

Jamie was a known quantity since he had been in our school last year as a three-year-old. It had been a hard year for Jamie. He is the youngest by far in his family. His older siblings are in high school and college. Jamie is a child who is in almost constant motion. Even at rest time, while lying on his back, he contorts his body into a variety of positions. Jamie claims to know everything but often talks in non sequiturs. At meeting time, while we were talking about not taking blocks from other people's buildings and respecting each other's work, he talked about bank robbers and bows and arrows. He is the child who on the first day of school socked the butterfly cage with a resounding blow for no apparent reason.

Jamie has his calmer moments, too. He enjoys listening to stories with the group after rest time. He often requests the teacher to read him a story all by himself. Jamie has sharp auditory skills. By mistake, I reversed two words while reading him a familiar story, and he called it to my attention. Then, on purpose, I substituted "Polly" for "Patty," and he picked that up as well.

Jamie needs lots of individual attention. I have to remind him to stay and finish cutting up the apple slices for our baked apple dish. He needs to know that he can be successful. He needs to be told that he is appreciated when he stirs those apple slices with a large wooden spoon after sprinkling them with cinnamon and sugar. I complimented him when he built a tower of brightly colored plastic pieces that fitted together easily. I also complimented him when he did a painting at the easel and when he made a fall collage with bittersweet and red sumac leaves on cardboard covered with tan burlap.

When Jamie's mother filled out the forms at parent orientation, she wrote, "Jamie has become extremely active. I would like him to be encouraged to attend to a project (any project). His attention span seems to be very short." I sensed a kind of quiet desperation with her comment within the parentheses. Nevertheless, she was recognizing that there was a problem, telling us that there was trouble. I don't know yet how to define the problem. It is still too early in the year. My approach to evaluation will be to listen and observe.

Jamie announced one morning last week that he wanted to be called "James" when he is at school. He told us that it was alright to be called Jamie at home, but at school he wanted his real name used. What was he telling us? Was his request to use his real name an indication that he wanted to be more grown up and have a grown-up name? Perhaps. I alerted his last year's teacher, our director, our music specialist, our dance specialist, the teacher in charge of calling out the names for carpool, and the remaining staff. I talked about it with the other children, and we agreed to start using the new name. At his suggestion I made a new "James" card for our juice and cracker chart and a new card for his section of the painting file. Before school one morning, as I was in the process of printing his name in red on the bright yellow circle to mark his cubby, he entered the room but didn't notice what I was doing. I quickly taped his "James" name tag on his cubby. Not more than two seconds later he looked up in that direction and his whole face lit up. "Thanks for changing my name," he said.

Evaluation begins with listening and observing and then acting on what one has heard and seen. The most important thing to remember about evaluation is that it is an on-going process that respects childhood and the individual child.

Some important questions to ask yourself are:

1. Have you created a nonthreatening environment for communicating evaluative comments to your co-workers?
2. When communicating with your co-worker, who initiates most of the discussions?
3. Have you set up a regular weekly meeting with your co-worker to discuss both your work and the progress of individual children?
4. Do you let your co-worker know when she has done a good job?
5. How do you invite criticism of your own work?
6. Have you compared the amount of time you spend listening to the time you spend talking?
7. Are your anecdotal records up to date?
8. Have you reread all available reports about the children in your class?
9. Would you be willing to arrange your schedule for an early morning or evening conference in order to have both parents there?

A PARENT CONFERENCE

I have just completed my initial round of parent conferences, which I look upon as a listening time and a learning time. I want to make parents feel welcome and at home. One way I do this, when the conference is scheduled at noon, is to invite the parent to have lunch with me. Today Kate's mother, Mrs. Moran, joined me for a luncheon conference.

On one of our small rectangular tables, I had set out two place settings using seashell-pattern paper plates in tones of tan, coordinated tan and white napkins, and white plastic forks, knives, and spoons. Completing the setting were brown pottery mugs made by my daughter in her early years as a potter, before she turned to working with porcelain. The menu included a wheel of baby Swiss cheese on a Swedish serving board, whole grain rolls, tofu egg salad, a seafood salad, and homemade ratatouille. For dessert was a basket of Seckle pears and McIntosh apples from my own orchard, along with decaffeinated and regular coffee. All this created a relaxed atmosphere for discussing Kate's behavior.

I was taught that you should start a parent conference by talking about a child's positive qualities. Over the years I have come to believe differently. Now I start the conferences by posing a simple question: "Tell me what your child is saying about school." I want parents to have free rein to talk at length about their own child. As a parent, I know that I know my child better than anyone else in the world. As a teacher, I respect what I hear. As a teacher, I have much to learn.

Of course, I had done my homework. I had looked over all the written reports on Kate from last year. I had read the "Your Child" form completed by her parents from both last year and this year and noted changes. I had talked to her former teachers, my assistant, and the school's director. I reread my notes on Kate in my notebook. I had thought long and hard about Kate's behavior in the classroom.

Mrs. Moran began by telling me that mornings often do not start out well for Kate. She does not always want to come to school and would prefer to stay at home with her mother. Kate has two older brothers, ages 6 and 7, whom Mrs. Moran described as being into "every imaginable mischief." Both Kevin and Richard are very physical, engaging in a lot of rough and tumble play which often gets out of control. There is a lot of pushing, shoving, punching, and kicking, a lot of name calling. In retaliation Kate has taken to biting.

Mrs. Moran appeared somewhat overwhelmed and wanted to talk at length about Kevin and Richard. Because she felt their aggressive behavior was having a profound effect on Kate, it was important that we talked about the two boys at this time. From the conference we came to understand why Kate needed time to "just look around" first thing in the morning rather than having a work plan as her classmates did. We came to understand why she had such a hard time focusing on her work at school. We came to understand why Kate pushed, shoved, kicked, and bit other children in school. We came to realize how hard it must be to be the youngest in the family.

In talking with Mrs. Moran I was able to reinforce the importance of observing the ground rules we have established for nursery school: A child needs to stop and think before striking someone. A child needs to know he or she can ask for help if it is needed. A child needs to understand that we work things out with words, not fists.

Among other things, we talked about the need for quiet family times at the end of the day for reading a book together, for listening to stories that a seven-year-old and a four-year-old can both enjoy, stories that can help to bind a family together. Finally, we talked about what Kate liked to do in school, how much she enjoyed making pumpkin pie and transplanting shoots from the impatience plant. Mrs. Moran left with several ideas to follow up on at home.

Parent conferences are a vital part of our school program. They are, more than anything, an opportunity for sharing and learning. Some are scheduled as early as 7:30 a.m. before a parent goes to work. Some are scheduled in the evening so both parents can be there. I have had conferences that lasted only 10 minutes, when the only counsel I could offer was, "You are a sensitive and caring parent. Keep on doing what you are doing." I also have had conferences that went on for an hour or more when a parent unburdened her concerns about the tensions in the family created by having an aging grandparent living in the home, or when a young mother shared her frustration over her husband's lack of interest in their children. Anything uppermost on a parent's mind is worthy of conference time, if it has a bearing on a child's well-being.

We, as teachers, are there not to offer pat answers but to listen, to share what we see and hear, and to suggest. Sometimes we are there just to tell Kate's parents what is going on in school, because Kate doesn't tell them and they would like to know.

As a teacher I look forward to each parent conference. I look forward to gaining new insights into a child from the parents' perspective. I look forward to sharing with parents some anecdote about their child. I look forward to telling Kate's mother that Kate recently said to me, "I have two things to tell you: I miss my mommy and I love you." As a teacher I know that I have much to learn. As a teacher I respect what I hear.

The most important thing about a parent conference is conveying an attitude of concern and working as a partner with the parents.

Some important questions to ask yourself are:

1. Have you clarified in your own mind what you want to accomplish at your first meeting with parents?
2. Have you provided a comfortable setting for the meeting?
3. Have you considered serving some refreshments without overburdening yourself?
4. Have you determined what the optimal length of time for the conference should be? How will you make that limit clear?
5. Are there specific questions you want to ask parents that will help you better understand their child?
6. Do you have direct quotes from the child to use as examples of his thinking?
7. Would you consider asking parents to organize and participate in a class project?
8. What can you do to end the conference on a positive note?

9. Have you been as good a listener at the parent conference as you try to be in the classroom?
10. Have you considered inviting a parent to bring his child to the next conference?

DECISION MAKING

My younger son, Thomas, attended a nontraditional prep school that offered a course in decision making. At the time I remember feeling that such a course very possibly could be the most important he took in his whole academic career, and very likely it was. I like to think that at The Nursery School we are offering such a course, too.

For four- and five-year-olds, most decisions are made by the adults in their lives, and understandably so. There are a multitude of decisions beyond their knowledge and experience that parents, grandparents, older siblings, doctors, teachers, babysitters, friends, and relatives make in order to guide and protect the young child. However, there are many decisions that young children are fully capable of making that adults make for them in the name of expediency. It does not have to be this way at nursery school.

At school we have the luxury of a different time frame. Although we, too, have schedules, the circumstances are different. We don't have to be on time for a dental appointment or a music lesson or meet grandma for lunch at precisely 12:15 p.m. We have more leeway with time and can be quite relaxed. However, we can and do make a very conscious effort to provide appropriate decision-making experiences for young children throughout the day. My long-range plan for the year, one that might seem impossible in September, is that by spring the children will be able to take over and efficiently carry out most of the major routines and leadership roles in the classroom, and that they will enjoy doing so.

We begin our day with a "worktime." When the children arrive, there is an attractive art project already set up on the table that seats eight. On the smaller table that seats six, there might be a cooking project with all the ingredients for pumpkin bread

40

ready to mix or the materials for a sink-and-float experiment (plastic tub of water, craft sticks, paper clips, and sponges) ready to use.

Our other room is filled with building blocks, and on top of the block shelf are wooden cars, trucks, boats, planes, and wooden people waiting to be used. There are also larger toys and seats with steering wheels, each waiting for a young driver. In the housekeeping corner are nylon nightgowns, a bridal hat, high heels, gold jewelry, and a black shoulder-strap bag; also shaving brushes, striped neckties, vests, jackets, engineer hats, hard hats, and wing-tipped shoes. In the play kitchen are a table and three chairs, a 1930s-style child's toaster with two cardboard slices of bread, and a dozen plastic eggs. In the science corner is a guinea pig, three red efts, four skinks, wooly bears galore, chrysalids, two very small toads, and more.

From the moment the children come through the door, there are a variety of possibilities to choose from. There are decisions to be made. Settling into work is easier for some than others. For this year's group, it has not been easy because of the wide range of abilities and experience within the group; several children seem to lack focus. My strategy this year is that as soon as the children are all assembled, I pick up the autoharp and start to strum and sing, "Will anyone whose name starts from A to Z follow follow follow me to the meeting place, because it's meeting time?" I usually begin by asking if anyone has seen anything that is different in the room. This tests their visual awareness and helps them to focus on the materials available and ultimately to make that first big decision. Then I ask, "What do you want to do today; what is your plan?" If a child has a hard time making a choice, I tell him to put on his thinking cap, or his work hat, and give him more time to make a decision. Then, if necessary, I offer some options; but each child will start the morning with a plan.

There is decision making at cleanup time, when they all line up and I sing and ask, "Joshua, you are number (and he says one). What's to be done number one?" and "Janie, you are number (and she says two). What will you do number two?" They love showing that they know their numbers. They know they will be given time to think about what their job is. If need be, I remind them to have their jobs at the tip of their tongue so that we can move right along. The children also are learning that decision making can be fun.

41

There is decision making after our juice and cracker chart is sung each day. Five children can select their jobs for the following day; it might be passing out the cups, the crackers, or passing out the large measuring cups filled with orange juice. They make their own decisions. There is decision making each day with the art materials, usually without any supervision. The results are quickly there for the young artist to behold. Constructing a box collage from fat, skinny, tall, and short boxes of every description can be a very satisfying decision.

Later on in the year, children will select stories to be read at rest time or records to be listened to during the morning. When children go visiting to another classroom, they decide where they want to go, and how long they want to stay. It's a big-time thing to do once they are comfortable enough in their own room.

My assistant, Ann, tested an apple muffin recipe at home. She brought the muffins to school. I thought they were terrible — too moist, on the mushy side, and no predominant flavor. I was in favor of pitching them out. She thought they were passable. Suddenly I had an idea. How about letting the children sample Ann's muffins and then decide whether we should make them in class. That's exactly what we did. I wrote two words on the board: "YUK" and "YUM." This was our first democratic vote of the school year, and both Ann and I were included in the balloting. The YUMS won by a narrow margin, so the very next day we plunged ahead with some minor alterations in the recipe: orange extract replacing the orange juice called for in the original recipe and six tablespoons of sugar, which Ann had forgotten to include in her recipe. We baked the muffins in smaller tins. After the next round of sampling, we repeated the vote and the YUMS won by a large majority, with only two dissenters. Now, with this first experience of opinion polling as a way of making a democratic decision, we can tackle more difficult issues. And we will!

There are so many other decisions that come up during school: decisions to try a waldorf salad for the very first time, decisions to drop down to the ground from the highest rung of "The Magic Carpet" climbing apparatus on the playground, decisions to be alone in the book corner and quietly thumb through a book if the morning didn't start too well. There also can be decisions to cry or to try not to, decisions to ask questions when you're not

The "doctor" of the day gives his new "patient" a hug.

quite sure, decisions to be angry if there aren't enough sprinkles on the chocolate icing of your birthday cupcake.

I like to think that at my school we are giving children an opportunity to grow. I like to think that we are offering a course in decision making. The most important thing to remember about decision making is that it fosters growth toward independence.

Some important questions to ask yourself are:

1. Do you consider independent decision making to be too complicated for four-year-olds to undertake?
2. How do you establish an expectation for young children to feel capable of making many decisions?
3. Do you structure the use of materials in the classroom in ways that allow the children to participate in decision making?
4. How can you simplify the decision-making choices so they are appropriate for young children?
5. Have you considered the technique of answering a question with a question in order to promote decision making?
6. Do you let the children know that decision making can often be difficult?
7. Can you admit to the children that on occasions you have made a "wrong" decision and need to change your mind?
8. How can you increase the complexity of decision making as the year progresses?
9. How will you communicate to parents about the importance you give to decision making, so that there will be consistency and carryover into the home?

THE YOUNGEST CHILD IN THE CLASS

Emily is the youngest child in our class. This would not be readily apparent until you had spent some time observing her in the classroom. At first you might notice her sun-bleached blond hair, her pale complexion, and her deep blue eyes that crinkle up each time she smiles. But soon you become aware that her thumb is often in her mouth. And when she speaks, her voice is just above a whisper. Emily is an endearing child but functions at a less mature level than her classmates.

Last year in the three-year-old class, Emily had had a difficult time separating from her mother; her mother had a hard time letting go of her little girl. There were tears and whimpers each morning when her mother left, even though she had spent the first month of school staying in the classroom with Emily. Emily seemed to need a lot of adult closeness throughout the day. She loved to sit on the teacher's lap or to press close against her side as she listened to familiar stories. Emily was most comfortable surrounded by soft things. She often could be found cuddled up on the soft pillows in the book corner or hugging her favorite soft lamb she brought from home each day. There were only a few things that Emily liked to do. She liked to play at the sandtable, pouring sand from one plastic container to another. She enjoyed juice and crackers at snack-time.

Emily's former teachers had serious doubts as to whether she should have been in school as a three-year-old. It had been a hard year for this retiring little girl.

When I arrived for my customary home visit in September, Emily was lying on the couch in the living room, covered with a light blanket. Her eyes were closed. Her mother said that she was not feeling well. I stayed and chatted about summer things — about swimming, making sand castles, eating ice cream — trying to touch a responsive chord in the small sleeping beauty. My talk was all in vain; Emily's eyes remained closed. After 20 minutes I said goodbye and returned to my car. Glancing out my rear-view mirror, I saw Emily happily waving goodbye from the front door. Somehow my leave-taking had brought forth a miraculous recovery!

This year Emily has successfully negotiated the separation from her mother, but those deep blue eyes still are often filled with tears. Emily has a hard time understanding that she can't have everything she wants when she wants it. She wants a second story read just as the first is being finished. She wants a fourth wheat wafer even before finishing the third. On the playground there are often tears waiting for her turn on the swing. In the classroom there are sometimes tears waiting for a chance to hold our guinea pig. There are occasional whimpers if someone else is wearing her favorite bridal hat. From time to time the corners of her mouth go down when waiting for her mother, who is near the end of the carpool line. Learning to wait has been a hard thing for Emily to do.

Emily likes to sit in our rocking chair and hold the guinea pig on her lap. Sitting there she can watch all the activity in the block room, listen to all the plans that are going on, and still keep her distance. Sitting there watching and listening, she is learning and gaining confidence to move closer to the group, when she feels the time is right. Right now it is still important for her to keep her distance.

I have seen Emily climb on our wooden playhouse and call for help because she couldn't figure out how to get down. I have heard Emily say that she cannot build with blocks because she cannot reach them. I have heard Emily say that she cannot pick up a red eft because her fingers are "too soft." I have observed Emily waving her hands in the air waiting for someone to help her put on her jacket. I have seen Emily lying on her back on the floor while two of her classmates wrestled to put on her snow boots. For Emily, it is more blessed to receive!

I have watched Emily work with the colored cubes, trying to replicate the simplest pattern. I have seen the struggle, have heard the teacher's words of encouragement, and have witnessed the sweet smile of success on Emily's face. There was much excitement in the classroom when Emily completed that task. I have seen her sitting with the wood-framed rectangle of brightly colored mushroom tiles, attempting to match the tiles on top. There was more excitement when the mushroom tiles were finally matched, and Emily could show her classmates what she was able to do.

Perhaps our expectations for Emily were too high. Perhaps we have been too hasty in comparing Emily with her peers. Perhaps we should begin to think more positively about those few accomplishments we have seen. Perhaps we should consider the amount of growth that has taken place since last year and be pleased. Perhaps we should remind ourselves that Emily is the youngest child in the class. Perhaps her parents will give her the gift of another year of nursery school. Each child is different, different in so many ways.

The most important thing to remember about the youngest child in the class is to accept her where she is and gently encourage her to grow.

Some important questions to ask yourself are:

1. At parent orientation did you talk about the variety of individual needs on the first few days of school?
2. Have you considered sharing the same kind of information with the children?
3. Are your expectations flexible enough so that each child can experience success?
4. Are there some children who will require a greater share of the teacher's attention?
5. Have you mapped out a series of mini-goals that the youngest child in the class can achieve?
6. Have you encouraged the youngest child in the class to take on new responsibilities?
7. Are you making every effort to keep the atmosphere of the classroom noncompetitive?
8. Do you remind yourself that praise is positive reinforcement?
9. Do you continually remind yourself that children mature at a different rate?
10. Have you talked to the parents of the youngest child in the class about the possibility of another year of nursery school?

HIGH SPIRITS AND HOLIDAYS

It is early December and already holiday spirits are runnning high. It seems that no sooner is the Thanksgiving turkey finished, then it's time to turn to activities for Christmas and Chanukah. It is almost a month of building excitement — a very long time for four-year-olds.

My feeling about school holiday celebrations for young children is the less the better. Simplicity is the key. We do have a Christmas tree brought in the last week before vacation and placed in the hall so that children and teachers and parents can all share in its splendor. We also have a holiday party the day before vacation begins, which lasts about an hour. Parents and siblings are invited.

For our party we arrange our three tables into a "T" shape and use red and green construction paper in an alternating pattern as placemats. Bold red, white, and green tulip pattern paper plates adorn each placemat, along with small red and green paper napkins. For this special day we serve apple juice rather than the routine orange juice. Clear plastic cups are filled with M&M's and silver, red, and green wrapped Hershey Kisses, leftovers from our candyland houses that were made the day before. Down the middle of the table are white paper plates filled with holiday cookies the children have made. Fresh green sprigs of yew fill in the empty spaces on the tables. At each child's place is a wrapped candy cane.

When the children arrive on party day, many are dressed for the special occasion with their "Mary Jane" shoes or a bright bow tie. The teachers don skirts and sweaters — no blue jeans for the party. As soon as everyone has gathered, the children sit down at the table and have their juice and cookies and the special candy treats. Extra places are set for siblings so they, too, can join in the party. The top of one of our storage shelves serves as a counter from which the parents attending the party can help themselves to our cookies and farm-fresh cider. Usually, some blockbuilding goes on. There must be some activity; you can't expect young children to stand around and chit-chat like adults at a cocktail party. On occasion, I read a story if I feel the group needs pulling together. Generally, they manage quite well with just the blocks.

It is an exciting time for the children as they come bearing gifts — often homemade goodies in colorful wrapping or a purchased gift with a card the child has made. Sometimes I am presented with a drawing. There is much excitement in that giving. After about 30 minutes of enjoying our refreshments at the table, we all go into our large motor room, where our music specialist joins us. She leads us in singing familiar songs — the rainy-day favorite "Pitter Patter," the rollicking "She'll Be Coming Around the Mountain" and "Jingle Bells," ending with a farewell chorus of "We Wish You a Merry Christmas and a Happy New Year."

These children are enjoying a story at their stuffed animal birthday party.

By the time the children have returned to the classroom after singing, the tables have been cleared. On them now are the candy-land houses and Christmas tree ornaments, which the children have made earlier in the week and can now take home. It is a happy ending, simple and short. But a lot has happened prior to the party, particularly the last week of school, that makes the party special for the children.

In December when Chanukah comes, we set up a "golden" menorah in the classroom, and each day we light the candles. It is a quiet way of celebrating the Jewish Festival of Lights, which is part of the heritage of some of our children. We light the candles when the shades are drawn and the lights are turned off during the children's rest time. Candles burning in a darkened room have a certain magic for all children. We also make potato latkes our cooking project for the week. Since we try to cook once a week all year long, this activity fits into our schedule naturally.

I am not big on glitter but I know the children are. At the beginning of the week prior to the holiday vacation, we do an art activity the children love. I cut the bottom of egg cartons into twelve sections. The children poke a hole in the center of a section with a pencil and insert a pipe cleaner, which serves as a hanger. Then the real fun begins as the children paint their "bells" and then go over to the folding cart where there are five or six bowls of different colored glitter from which to choose. There the children can sprinkle glitter to their hearts' content. We hang the glittering bells to dry on a string stretched across the room. Seeing their bells on display pleases our young artists and often spurs some of our reluctant artists to try their hand at bell making. When the bells are dry, the artists hang them on the Christmas tree.

Another holiday art activity we do is a simple paper-cutting project. All that is needed is a pair of scissors and half a piece of colored construction paper. I demonstrate to the children how to turn and cut and turn and cut but without cutting to the edge. It is a simple process but one that takes a goodly amount of concentration. It creates a colorful spiral decoration, which we hang on the string that is stretched across our room.

The last week of school before vacation is also the time we make our holiday cookies. This is a two-day project. On the first day we make the dough and roll it into 90 small balls, which are refrigerated overnight. On the second day comes the shaping and the decorating with sprinkles. The baking is done right in the classroom, allowing the children to experience the whole baking process and using their senses to enjoy what they have created. Having a portable oven in the school has been a real boon, even though we can bake only small amounts at a time.

The day before our party we make our candyland houses. My first job is to collect half-pint milk containers from one of the local public schools and wash them out. Next, I staple the tops shut and put each one in the center of a white square cardboard with a border of red. The children and I then mix up a big batch of "icing glue" made with egg whites and confectioners' sugar, which is portioned into several small bowls for use by individual children. I give the children baskets of graham crackers, which have been cut to size to serve as the sides and the roof of the house. After all the the houses are "boarded up," the decoration begins with various candies provided in plastic cups. Each house is different — some with gardens and a bench, some with paths to the front door, some with two chimneys. Some houses are for simple folk; others are done in a style fit for a king and a queen. Each child's candyland house reflects an individual artistic expression. After the party the children can take their houses home to savor or to save. This project has great appeal for all the children.

Sometime in December the children and I make bird feeders constructed from two styrofoam cups. One cup is inverted over the other, serving as a canopy to keep the birdfeed dry when it rains or snows. A thick pipe cleaner holds the cups together and also serves as a hanger. The bottom cup has a cutout opening with a perch below it on which a bird can stand and peck at the seeds inside. The children take their bird feeders home at vacation time with instructions to hang them in a place where birds are likely to gather. This project serves two objectives. It gives children a sense of responsibility for protecting wildlife by providing food in the cold weather. It also serves as a reminder of the bridge between school and home. Vacations take children away from a world they love. Vacations can be a long wait.

I like to write the children a note during vacation. Sometimes it's a thank-you note for their gift, but I also use the occasion to remind them of the good times we had at our party and that I am looking forward to seeing them back at school. I use my notes to ask a few questions or make a simple statement: "Wasn't that a nice holiday party that we had?" "I think everyone enjoyed the holiday cookies you helped to make." "Will you make an angel in the snow in your backyard during vacation?" "Will you make a block building with an entrance and an exit when you come back to school?" Bird feeders and notes are tangible ways of reminding children that school will start again soon, and we will all be back together.

During December, even with the excitement of making our room and tree decorations, baking our cookies, and constructing our candyland houses, I try to maintain the normal, low-key classroom climate. When a particular holiday project is done, I put out the playdough, table blocks, or puzzles — activities associated with the regular classroom routines. We talk about the excitement of the holidays, and I acknowledge the children's high spirits; but I remind the children that we are still in school and we have work to be done. It helps to settle things down. I also feel it is important to have the children spend as much time as they can out of doors. They need time to siphon off some of their energy. They need space to run and climb and talk in loud voices, too.

In December holiday spirits run high. The most important thing to remember about high spirits and holidays is to keep the celebrations simple.

Some important questions to ask yourself are:

1. Can you downshift your own holiday activities in order to retain a low-key atmosphere in the classroom?
2. Can you make a three-week plan in order to spread out the holiday activities?
3. In talking with the children about the excitement of the holidays, will you give them plenty of time to talk about what is going on at home?
4. Have you thought about holiday art activities that require lots of involvement?
5. Will you have waterplay and playdough available as a calming influence?
6. If spirits are running too high, would you call the children together and ask them what they think might be most helpful for them?
7. Have you thought about increasing the structure of your program as vacation time draws nearer?

8. Are you planning to have more time for out-of-door physical activity than usual?
9. Will you or the school director send a message to the parents wishing them a happy holiday and urging them to keep their celebration simple?
10. Have you considered some way of staying in communication with your class over the holiday break that is not too burdensome?

FRIENDSHIP: TEACHER TO TEACHER

One of the most important things we adults can do for young children is to model the kind of person we would like them to be. Living together for five mornings a week at school gives teachers that opportunity. With the interaction and decision making that goes on when there are two or more teachers in the classroom, I try to establish a cooperative spirit that permeates the classroom. I want the children to see the camaraderie between the other teachers and me. I want them to see a supportive and caring relationship and a sense of enjoyment in our work together. I want the children to treat their peers the same way I treat my peers.

My school, The Nursery School, Westchester Ethical Humanist Society in White Plains, New York, has four classrooms, with a head teacher and an assistant teacher in each room. Our school has been in existence for 23 years. One of our head teachers has been here since the school's founding. One assistant teacher has been there for 20 years. This is my nineteenth year as a head teacher working with four- and five-year-olds. Our school is a cohesive unit. For me, it is a home away from home. It is a place of both comfort and stimulation, a place that offers aesthetic satisfactions, constant challenges, and continual growth — much like a family in a home.

About 10 years ago, our staff did an unusual thing, which tells a lot about our priorities, about working together, and about friendship, too. It was the consensus of the head teachers that there was too great a discrepancy between the pay scale of the head teachers and the assistant teachers, despite the differences in training, experience, and educational backgrounds. That year, the head teachers decided that their salary increment should go to their assistants, thus narrowing the gap in salaries. Over the years we all have benefited from that decision.

When I work with a new assistant teacher, I have a plan in my mind that evolves over the first six weeks. I observe whether she feels comfortable in the jobs she is undertaking. I observe the pace at which she works, paying particular attention to her sense of timing. I want to see how she anticipates the needs of the children. I want to see how she interprets the mood of the group. Just as I do with the children in my class, I spend a lot of time just listening and observing. I try to plan opportunities that will encourage personal growth and professional development. For me, this is what makes each school year different. It forces me to stretch my mind, and it sharpens my sensitivity to others.

A few years ago while attending the annual potluck supper for the Westchester Association for the Education of Young Children, I sat across from a woman I had never met before. When I asked about her work, she told me that she was involved in a program at the Bank Street College of Education in New York City called "Follow Through." I was intrigued with what she told me since I had done my first master's degree at Bank Street many years ago, and the experience was a turning point in my life. Bank Street started me thinking in new ways. From that chance meeting, I decided to go back to school the very next month, after an absence of 17 years, to work on a second master's in supervision and administration.

The courses I took over a period of two-and-a-half years have expanded my horizons and have provided me greater depth in areas related to my work. As a result I feel that I have more to offer the children, their parents, and the teachers with whom I work. The desire to improve and change keeps one stimulated. All of this has a direct bearing on the quality of teaching that goes on in the classroom.

As a result of the courses I was taking, I was able to set up a more systematic training program for new assistant teachers in our school. In a series of meetings we discussed the various roles they could take over in the classroom and the evaluation procedures we could use in assessing how well they carried out those roles. We recorded the discussions so they could be used as a reference by the individuals involved and also for assistant teachers joining our staff in the future. The tapes have been a very helpful supervisory tool. In working with my own assistant teacher, we both are learning what each of us needs to do to fulfill our respective roles.

55

And as we worked together, the greater our respect for one another has grown. From that mutual respect has come friendship.

My way of working with my assistant is evident in the things we discuss and do before the children burst into the room at 9:00 a.m. The interchange we have sets the tone for the day. I need to know if everything is all right at her home — whether she needs to make some phone calls during the morning, whether she has to leave in a hurry at noon. We use this time together to share our thoughts about children and parents — what hasn't gone well and how it could go better, what children need individual attention, what small groups work well together. We share our thoughts about curriculum for today and for the days ahead.

My way of working with my assistant also is evident in the many things that happen after the children arrive in the morning. It is sharing the decision making so that she knows her opinion counts. It is giving her the opportunity to make decisions on her own. It is sharing ideas about an art project and letting her set it up on her own. It is sharing discussions with parents and answering phone calls that come in. It is sharing our observations about children at parent conferences. It is sharing the leadership roles in the classroom.

I feel about my co-worker the same way I feel about the children in the classroom. I want to create a supportive atmosphere that allows for individual expression, an atmosphere in which she is comfortable enough to take some risks. I want her to know that even though mistakes are made, they can be rectified.

I also think that it is important to know about your co-worker's life away from school. Just as I want my co-worker to know what my interests are and what matters most to me, I want to know about her homelife (if she wants me to), her husband and children, and the people who are important in her life. I want to know something of her commitments at home and in the community. I like to know what she is reading and to exchange books occasionally so we can discuss them. I like to share the brand name of a winter boot with a felt lining that will be comfortable for her on the playground or to recommend an excellent sushi restaurant. I like making connections. Connections are a part of what relationships are all about. Connections are a part of friendship.

There also are friendships among the other staff in the school. Ours is a staff that helps one another; we share our problems and solutions. We have an "open door" policy in our school that allows children to visit another classroom. It provides connections between children and other children, between children and other teachers, and between teachers and other teachers. We like to know how Karen managed herself in another group and what she found that interested her. We like to know that Eric demolished his block building just before his visiting time was over.

Our teachers do a lot of sharing. We loan books to each other's classroom and invite other teachers to see a wonderful art project that one of our mothers did with the children. When one of us brings our dog to school, it visits each of the classrooms. When our Monarch butterflies emerge, they go traveling too. Our guinea pig, Little Nose, may spend an hour across the hall, or I can invite one of the teachers into our class to do her special "Tickle Song" with feathers. Connections are a part of friendship.

One of the most important things we can do for young children is to model the kind of person that we would like them to be. I want the children to treat their peers the same way I treat my peers.

Some important questions to ask yourself are:

1. How well do you know your co-worker?
2. Are you supportive of your co-worker by listening to her ideas?
3. Have you set aside time each week, either before or after school, to talk together?
4. Have you set both short- and long-term goals for your co-worker?
5. Do you share responsibility and decision making with your co-worker?
6. Do you share information with your co-worker and the rest of the staff?
7. Have you made an effort to learn about the out-of-school life of your co-worker and other staff without invading their privacy?
8. Are you making an effort to become good friends with your colleagues?

HANDLING SENSITIVE ISSUES
IN THE CLASSROOM

A few years ago our staff decided that we would list the sensitive issues that had come up in our classrooms during recent years. We were taken aback at both the number and severity of crisis situations that had surfaced within our small school. On the list was the death of a grandparent, the death of a close relative, the death of an adult friend, parent separation and divorce, a sibling born with cancer, a family home destroyed by fire. The most difficult of all was the suspected suicide of a parent. The list went on to include other tragic events. It quickly became apparent that each year we were called on to work with the children and their families to help them cope with traumatic events.

I remember how shaken the staff, children, and their parents were when the space shuttle "Challenger" exploded and the seven astronauts died. This was a national tragedy, which the media covered in an exhaustive and relentless manner. It was an incident that affected each child in quite different ways.

We learned of the tragedy just after the children had left for home at 11:45 a.m. on January 28, 1986. As a staff, we were individually and collectively stunned. I have cousins living in Concord, New Hampshire, who were friends of Christa McAuliffe, the teacher in space. It brought the tragedy that much closer to me. I went home, listened to the radio, watched the television coverage, and thought about how the children would react. I wondered how I could help them to understand the great sadness we all were feeling. In working with young children, you have to reduce an experience to its simplest elements in order to bring it within their understanding. By doing this, you help yourself as well as the children.

That evening I had a call from one of my school parents to say that Jim "was fixated on the explosion." He wouldn't leave the television set, and he was asking for more and more information. I thanked Mrs. Douglas for calling. Forewarned, I felt forearmed.

The next morning the staff and the school director met and discussed our plans. The teachers of the three-year-olds were hesitant about bringing up the subject. They felt it should come from the children first. However, after some discussion, it was agreed that each teacher would handle it in her own fashion, but that the subject of the shuttle explosion should be introduced by the teachers. The director said she would write a covering letter about what our educational approach would be. The letter was to go home with the children the following day.

I had brought the morning copy of the *New York Times*, which had several excellent visuals of the space shuttle. For me, the visuals communicate more than words can, and even young children can relate to them. We had our regular morning meeting, but I changed the format. I started out by saying, "Something happened yesterday that made me very sad, and I want to talk with you about it." That is just what I did.

Jim was nearly exploding in his eagerness to tell what he knew about the space shuttle explosion. My job was to see that he did not dominate the discussion. There were 14 other children who needed to be heard. We talked about many things — about Christa McAuliffe, the teacher who was aboard the shuttle, about the names of the six other astronauts and what their jobs were. We talked about how soon the explosion took place after takeoff and about where the fire may have started. We talked about the fact that no one knew why it happened and about how people would try to find out what went wrong.

By asking each child to verbalize what he or she thought had happened, I would be able to clear up any misconceptions. I started with Jim. He said, "It has never happened before. I'm going to build (with blocks) the shuttle and the astronauts and make the sound of the explosion." Matthew said, "Nine people melted, and some fire got in the sky." Charles said, "Thunder could have struck it and burnt it." Samantha looked at the floor and said, "I don't know anything about it. I didn't see it on TV." Cathy added, "It was just like some of our butterflies died." John said, "The space shuttle blew up; it could blow up with a bow and arrow." Deborah ended our discussion by saying, "It's a very sad thing, but it doesn't usually happen. It's unusual."

I had decided before I came to school that perhaps we could simulate, in a small way, what the explosion did to the space shuttle and its passengers. I told the children that, if they wished, they could build a space shuttle out of blocks. And just prior to cleanup time, they could explode their shuttle. Today would be very different. We would abandon our usual practice of carefully unbuilding our structures. One at a time, the children, wearing their hard hats, demolished their space shuttles, while the other children stayed well out of reach of the falling blocks. This activity, using a familiar medium, gave the children a context for understanding the tragic accident.

Remembering how Samantha had looked down at the floor and said she didn't know anything about the accident, I decided to speak to her mother and urge her to share more information with Samantha about this national calamity everyone was talking about. This led to a lengthy discussion about the importance of making a child feel that she counts, that she is old enough to be aware of the world and is capable enough to process the information.

John's mother called our school director soon after John arrived home. She was furious. She felt it was inappropriate for the teachers to bring up the subject of the shuttle explosion. In her view it was the parents' responsibility to talk to their child about such a sensitive issue. I waited until very late in the afternoon to call. By then she was considerably calmer. I explained how our handling of the shuttle explosion was similar to how we handle the death of one of our school animals or any other traumatic situation that touches the life of a young child. I explained how we try to interpret such tragic events in concepts that are understandable to the four-year-old mind. She seemed to be able to accept that.

Three months later my *New York Times*, now slightly yellow with age, continued to serve as a visual aid in our room. We counted the number of astronauts who perished and learned their names. We looked at the photographs of the shuttle as the smoke started to envelope the craft and talked about it a lot. With blocks and thick cardboard tubes, the children have built and rebuilt and built again the ill-fated Challenger and dramatized its demise.

When dealing with sensitive issues with young children, it is necessary to focus on those elements that are within their understanding. Through calm discussion and dramatic play, children can both learn and have an outlet for their emotions. The most important things to remember about handling sensitive issues in the classroom is to consider the children's emotional needs and their level of maturity.

Some important questions to ask yourself are:

1. Have you met as a staff to share ideas about how to handle sensitive issues?

2. Have you considered inviting outside professionals to talk with the staff on how to deal with sensitive issues in the classroom?

3. Can you communicate to parents in a convincing manner your approach to handling sensitive issues in the classroom?

4. Have you thought through how you will explain a given sensitive issue to young children, including what materials are available to make your explanation more understandable? The "Open Family Series" by Sara Bonnett Stein, published by Walker and Company, is a good source for both teachers and parents. Some of the titles are *On Divorce, About Dying, The Adopted One, About Handicaps, A Hospital Story,* and *That New Baby.*

5. Have you read professional journals and other materials that give additional insights into how to handle sensitive issues with young children?

6. If you firmly believe that discussing a sensitive issue makes it less frightening to young children, are there any precautions you should take?

7. Have you carefully considered each child's emotional needs in order to be be as supportive as possible when sensitive issues arise?

TAKING RESPONSIBILITY

I firmly believe in having young children take responsibility — responsibility for possessions, for themselves, and for others. Taking responsibility doesn't just happen. There have to be people who want to see it happen. There have to be people who plan for it to happen. There have to be people who will praise a child when they see it happen. This means there have to be opportunities for children to take responsibility and expectations for them to behave responsibly.

There are so many ground rules for young children to learn — an incredible number of do's and don'ts. However, most children come to accept and live by the ground rules when their teacher takes the time to explain, in a simple way, why they are necessary.

One of the first things I ask children to do when they arrive in the morning is to hang up their jackets on the hook in their cubbies. This can be a bother to Andrew when he arrives and wants to work with his best buddy, who has already started building the "George Washington Bridge" with the quadruple unit blocks. Nevertheless, it's a responsibility that is his alone. When the snow begins to fall, and there are snowpants, jackets, scarves, mittens, and boots to contend with, that responsibility is still his. Things have to be put away so people don't trip over them.

Toys, books, and other items from home come to school on a regular basis. Sharing a favorite book from home, which the teacher reads to the whole group, is fairly easy. Not so easy is giving Janie a turn at using "Rainbow Bright," your pastel-colored plastic pony, when you really want to keep it all to yourself. But the rules have been spelled out and talked about: If you bring a toy to school, it's to be shared. And it's your responsibility to see that people get turns. If you just can't manage to do that, there is the option of keeping the toy in your cubby. Whichever way it goes, the responsibility is yours.

There are other responsibilities relating to the care of possessions. Not stepping on the small wooden sailboat when working in the block room and washing out the paintbrushes and storing them with their black bristles standing up are responsibilities. Not tearing the pages of *Mr. Rabbit and the Lovely Present* as you thumb through it and putting it back on the bookshelf are responsibilities. Children need to be aware that stepping on plastic forks in the housekeeping corner can crack them and dropping blocks on the floor while standing on a chair to "unbuild" a structure can splinter the edges. Children need to be aware that toys are made of different materials and that some are more durable than others. It's their responsibility.

Being responsible for oneself is much harder than being responsible for things. It requires more than putting things back neatly on the shelves at cleanup time. Being responsible for oneself is an all-day, everyday thing. In our small school of only 62 children, we allow them to visit friends in other classrooms because we feel it extends the range of their experiences. It is the child's responsibility to ask for permission to leave the classroom, and his responsibility to return when he says he will.

Children need to be responsible out on the playground, too. They need to know that they must stay on the playground and not go into the surrounding woods and not go near the parking lot. They need to know that if they leave the playground to use the bathroom or to get a drink at the water fountain, they must tell the teacher. It's their responsibility.

Children need to be responsible in how they move about the classroom. It means stepping over the "George Washington Bridge" instead of kicking it, stepping on it, or crashing into it. It means circling a floor puzzle that may be in the direct path to the housekeeping corner. It means being aware of where things are in the room at all times and plotting one's moves accordingly.

Children need to be responsible in how they use their own strength. They need to learn that the power in their arms and legs should be constructive, not destructive. They need to know that if a unit block is thrown, it can topple a building or hit a person and hurt that person. They need to know that throwing anything in the classroom is not allowed. It is their responsibility to remember this.

Children also must be responsible for the way they treat others. They need to know that what they say can affect other people in both good and bad ways. Words can make another person laugh or cry. They need to know that when they say, "You can't come to my birthday party!" it can make a person feel bad. They also need to know that when they say, "I had a delicious day!" it makes the teacher smile all over.

Taking responsibility doesn't just happen. There have to be people who want to see it happen. There have to be people who plan for it to happen. There have to be people who praise a child when they see it happen. And these people have to be responsible, too. The most important thing to remember about developing responsibility in young children is that it must be expected. And there must be multiple experiences for practicing responsibility so it becomes internalized in a child's thinking and behavior.

Some important questions to ask yourself are:

1. Do you model responsible behavior through your own actions in the classroom?
2. Do you repeatedly but gently remind children of what you expect them to undertake and accomplish?
3. Do you frequently use the phrase, "That's your responsibility," and make it stick?
4. Do you on occasion enlist the assistance of the class in helping a particular child assume responsibility? For example, you might say, "Jack has a hard time with cleanup, and we all need to help him do his share of the work."
5. Do you use praise for a job well done as a way to encourage children to be more responsible?
6. Do you ever feel like giving up on a child because you expend too much energy for too little results? How can you avoid this attitude?
7. From the parent conference have you learned about the child's responsibilities at home?
8. Do you have specific suggestions for parents about jobs that a child can do at home to develop a sense of responsibility?
9. Do you increase the amount of responsibility for children as the year progresses?

BLOCKBUILDING IS MORE THAN BUILDING WITH BLOCKS

One of the parents came in today to ask my advice on buying blocks for her daughter. This is a child who sleeps in curlers almost every night and wears hand-painted barrettes in her blond ringlets. This is a child whose parents dress her up in designer clothes and matching shoes at the slightest provocation. This is a child who has appeared on the television program, "The Magic Garden," and was taught, at the age of three, to recite the Pledge of Allegiance on cue.

This is a parent who places great stock in appearances. But this is a parent who listens to her child and her endless stories about her block buildings. This is a parent who understands the importance of blocks in her child's life.

We are four months into the school year, and the changes that have occurred in the blockbuilding area are truly impressive. The enthusiasm for blockbuilding escalates as the year progresses. It doesn't just happen; it's a planned escalation. Blocks have the highest priority in my classroom. I have built up a vast collection of blocks (270 unit-blocks alone), and I use part of my new equipment allotment to purchase a variety of sizes and shapes to fill in the gaps.

It is not only the quantity and variety of shapes that make the young architects want to build; it is also their placement on the shelves. Blocks should be stacked lengthwise on the shelves so the children can see their shape. Storage of blocks on the shelves should convey a definite sense of order at the beginning of each day and also at the end at cleanup time. To help children keep the blocks in order, I put on the back of block shelves white cardboard cards with black magic marker outlines of each of the different block shapes. These visual reminders help the children return the blocks to their proper place on the shelves. Such reminders are especially useful during the beginning days of school when the children are learning the housekeeping routines.

In a way, the space allotted to blocks tells how a teacher feels about blocks. Because I think blocks are an important learning tool, I give blockbuilding as much space as possible in my class-room — a 15-by-22-foot area. To provide easy access to the block shelves, I have put red Mystic tape on the floor two feet in front of the shelves to mark off the area where no building is to go on. If a block structure is started and then abandoned, I first ask permission and then put the blocks away in order to create addi-tional blockbuilding space. Having lots of uncluttered space in-vites young builders to get to work.

I think it's important to be present in the block area. If you really believe in blocks as a medium for growth, then you are there to ask and answer questions and to lend a hand. You are there to add a block to the top of a structure that a child can't reach. You are there to offer encouragement and praise when a child builds a particularly creative structure. Blockbuilding offers limitless possibilities, whether it's a variation on an old theme or an entirely new creation.

The accessories on top of the block shelf help to determine the direction the blockbuilding will take. These accessories should change as new ideas present themselves. Listening to the chil-dren's conversations and to their questions as they work helps to determine which accessories to add and which have outlived their usefulness.

At the beginning of the school year, I limit the accessories. I put out a bulldozer, an airplane, a dump truck, a gas station, a tugboat, a sailboat, and several small wooden cars. Gradually other accessories are added — some on request and others to spark a new interest — such as the wooden people, the flexible Flagg rub-ber family, train tracks and trains, and small wooden doll house furniture. And for decorative purposes there are colored cubes, also sturdy cardboard tubes of various sizes painted red or blue, and a quantity of two-by-fours painted red to simulate bricks.

One of the things the young builders like most is a sign that personalizes their building. For making signs I keep a basket filled with brightly colored construction paper, two magic markers, a roll of masking tape, and a pair of scissors near the chair where I sit. Having a sign that says, "Don't kick down or touch my building — Sarah," lets the world know just how important Sarah's structure is to her. Sometimes two or three children will discuss what kind of signs they want and how they will be attached to their structures. Sometimes signs are saved and put in the cubby for use the next day. Sometimes signs are taken home to use on home constructions.

Personalized signs are an integral part of our blockbuilding program. It makes the children proud to see their feelings about their building structures written down on paper and their names added in big bold letters. Some like signs so much they will request one even before they start to build. But they soon come to accept our rule: "Signs available only on completion of your work." Sometimes just the thought of a sign can be motivation enough to start building.

In addition we have small wooden signs: stop signs, railroad crossing signs, and one-way signs. We also have a roll of wallpaper printed with all kinds of signs: yield signs, deer crossing signs, and school signs. These can be cut out and mounted on cardboard with a tongue depressor as a stand.

Wearing hard hats adds a real-life dimension to blockbuilding, and they are a real protection. We have eight hard hats in the room — yellow ones, black ones, red ones, and white ones, picked up at flea markets or tag sales for 25 cents each. They are a bit too large for the children, but they love to wear them. We have a rule in the block room: "If you are working near or working on a tall building, one that is taller than you are, you must wear a hard hat." From experience I know that it's a good rule. Last year a skyscraper made of quadruple unit blocks toppled over on top of Frank. The crash still resounds in my ears as I remember Frank's frightened face when his structure fell on him. I was frightened, too. We were all grateful that he was wearing his yellow hard hat.

Later in the year, after the children have become adept at building structures, I introduce the idea of having an elevator in their buildings. Elevators are simple to make. All you need is a piece of wood the size of a double-unit block with a cup hook screwed into the center. This is placed across the top of a building. The elevator itself can be made out of juice cans, plastic containers, or a berry basket. I punch a hole on each side of the container, draw a string through the holes, and tie it roughly two inches above the top of the container. Then I measure out lengths of string for different size buildings and add large wooden beads at the end of the string to serve as a handle. By attaching one end of the string to the container, looping it over the cup hook, and then pulling on the other end, the "elevator" moves up and down with its load of wooden people or colored cubes. Children are fascinated with being an elevator operator, being in control of a moving object going to each floor of the "Empire State Building" or the "World Trade Center."

Blockbuilding offers many challenges to young children. At our morning meeting I might say, "I have a problem for you to solve today. See if you can figure out how to attach your building to your neighbor's." Or I might say, "See if you can make a path to the building nearest you." If three children are working together on a structure, I might ask, "See if you can work out where the entrance and the exit of your building will be." Children enjoy such challenges, and in the process they become familiar with new concepts and new vocabulary. For example, by pointing out the EXIT sign just above the door in our school, children can make the connection between the concept and the word. And it is an important word to know.

Another supplement to the blocks are thick cardboard cylinders of various lengths, which I have painted and repainted over the years. Cylinders can lead to new ways of thinking about building structures. They can act as water towers or smoke stacks or turrets on a castle. I also have a collection of various size wooden cylinders. Just today Thomas started talking about water pipes underneath the city. The box on the shelf containing small wooden cylinders came down, and in short order there were water pipes connecting two buildings. Perhaps tomorrow would be the appropriate time to visit the school's basement to see what kind of pipes are there. Trains and train tracks are another supplement to blocks. I prefer to have the children create their own tracks with blocks, because it allows them to be more creative when developing routes for the trains to travel on. By having the accessories readily available, they can be put to use on a moment's notice.

Last week we started our "Manhattan Project." Each year this project comes about in different ways. This year it began when two of the children started talking about lighthouses. This gave

Exploring the block area on the first day of school is a prelude to the creative structures these two will soon be building.

me material for our morning meeting. We talked about what lighthouses are made of, where they are located, and what equipment they have to have. Some of the children have been to lighthouses and climbed to the top. One child has never heard of a lighthouse. To clarify points as we talk, I use two pictures of lighthouses mounted on the wall in our block room.

I have collected a large supply of Quaker Oats boxes, both small and large, which make wonderful lighthouses. The round boxes are painted one day. Then the following day we put together the six-volt batteries with two wires and a bulb in a porcelain receptacle and mount it in the lighthouse. We can also add off-on switches so that the lighthouses can flash signals to the ships at sea. When the lighthouses are completed, we pull the shades and turn out the lights so we can see the flashing light in the dark. These are memorable moments for the young architects and the young scientists.

When the lighthouses are well under way, we start on "The Hudson River" and "The East River" components of our "Manhattan Project." We begin by moving two of our tables out into the hall in order to have plenty of floor space. Then we cover the floor with newspaper and roll out two 8-foot strips of brown craft paper on top of the newspapers. Then the painting begins. First the children must decide what color they want to make the water. Some request blue with white, some ask for blue with a little yellow; some want blue with a few drops of red. The variety of colors creates interesting effects. The children use either three-inch foam brushes or the regular one-inch, long-handled brushes they use every day at the easel. With the foam brushes, the river is smooth and flowing, and the painting is completed in a matter of a few minutes. I prefer that the children use the regular brushes, even though it takes longer to cover the expanses of paper with paint. The children seem to enjoy the involvement with painting spread over a longer time period. They engage in more conversation and problem solving, and the river seems to belong more to them.

We use many accessories in the block area while doing the "Manhattan Project." We make all kinds of boats — sailboats made from the top section of an egg carton with a craft stick and a paper sail inserted in the middle, styrofoam fire boats and barges, rowboats and "engine" boats made from different sizes and shapes of boxes. Each boat has its own string so it can be pulled up and down the river. The children make bridges to span the river and all kinds of paper fish to swim in the water. The fish have paper clips attached to their mouths. Soon the young fishermen line the banks of the river with bamboo poles, a string line, and a magnet attached as bait to catch the fish. Fishing is good on the "East River" and the "Hudson River."

I like to take photographs of the "Manhattan Project" with the children posing beside their block structures. It reminds them of what they have done in the past and shows them how their work has changed over the year. Sometimes we leave buildings up overnight, particularly in the spring when the good weather beckons us outdoors. And we skip our rest time, which normally takes place in the block area. Leaving up your building means your work is worthwhile. It means that your work is prized for its individuality and creativity.

The most important thing to remember about blocks is that they are a medium that helps young children to grow as individuals and as group members. Blockbuilding presents many opportunities for problem solving and decision making.

Some important questions to ask yourself are:

1. Do I have a plan for using blocks related to activities in the fall, in the winter months, and in the spring?
2. Have I allotted enough space for blockbuilding?
3. Do I have enough blocks for my age group?
4. Do I have shelves to store the blocks in an orderly fashion at the end of each day?
5. Have I established ground rules for working in the block area?
6. Do I have a set of blockbuilding problems that will challenge the children?
7. What accessories do I have on hand to enhance the blockbuilding activity?
8. What accessories should I be collecting for blockbuilding?
9. Is there a camera in the classroom to photograph the children and their buildings?

MUSIC IN THE CLASSROOM

As a youngster, I took piano lessons for seven years but never played very well. The truth of the matter is that my teacher, Wanda Labunski, made the most delicious Dobach torte that I had ever tasted; and I knew that at the end of my lesson I would be offered a piece. I do not play the piano anymore. In fact, my musical talent is quite limited; but my classroom is filled with music. My primary instrument is my voice. I also strum the autoharp. It is a great instrument for getting the children's attention. The moment that I begin to strum, the children know that something special is about to happen.

Each day as my first official act I use the autoharp to call everyone together for meeting time. Usually just one strum is all it takes to bring everyone to our meeting spot. If there are a few stragglers, I give them some extra time by singing about those children who are already sitting down. At times I might need to add, "I need Sarah and I need Ned to come sit down for our meeting time." Then, when everyone's name has been sung and all are present, we start our early morning dialogue.

In addition to using the autoharp to call the children to meeting time, I use it to dramatize points during the meeting. By strumming and voice inflections, I can create an air of mystery or an air of excitement. The children soon come to understand a wide range of meanings, which I communicate with my voice and body language. Our meeting ends with my singing and asking the children how they want to start the morning. When I strum and sing, "Now everyone has a plan," the children know the meeting is terminated and it is time to go to work.

I also use the autoharp at the end of an activity period to indicate that it is cleanup time. I strum and sing, "What would you like to do today. What would you like to put away?" After the

72

children decide what they want to do for cleanup time and every-one has a job, I strum the notes F, G, and C and ask the children to join me in singing, "Now everyone has a job." We have reached closure and are working as a group. When the children have fin-ished cleanup, they can go on to the next pleasurable activity — juice and crackers.

At snack time we do responsive singing from the very first day of school. I sing the names and jobs of the children assigned to preparing the snacks — passing out the cups, setting out the crack-ers in three baskets, and setting out the juice in large measuring cups that serve as pitchers. The children respond by repeating what I have sung. For the few children for whom responsive sing-ing is difficult, I offer support by singing along with them until they are able to respond on their own. Through responsive sing-ing the children are learning to listen to their own voice and the voices of their classmates. They are learning that it is necessary to stop talking in order to hear their own name sung. They are learning that singing is fun, and that we all do it a little different-ly. Toward the end of the year I ask the children if they would like to take turns being the teacher and sing to the group as I do. The child stands on a chair facing the group; I stand nearby ready to whisper a child's name in case the "teacher" forgets it. Most of children manage quite well being "teacher."

The rest period is a quiet time, a change of pace after juice and crackers and before going out to the playground. I sing to relax the children as they stretch out on their brightly colored mats to rest. I sing softly to each child by name and then to all the animals in our room: "I like the way our two toads are resting, now everyone is resting quietly."

I also like to share old songs that I learned as a child. We sing old favorites like, "L-O-L-L-I-P-O-P" or "Daisy, Daisy." The children love to sing these songs over and over, and we do. We also have a record player, tape player, and a good collection of records and tapes. Our portable radio is set for the New York City public broad-casting station or the jazz station out of Stamford, Connecticut, depending on my mood and the mood in the classroom. We also have instruments, which we bring into the classroom. Sometimes parents volunteer to come to school and play the cello, violin, or guitar. Occasionally one of the children will give a brief "recit-al" of some of the songs learned at home.

Most of all, I want children to become aware of the beauty of different sounds and of their effect on our feelings. I want them to be aware of the sound of bird calls, the sound our guinea pig makes when you scratch her back, the sound a cricket makes as he rubs his back wings together. The rhythm of these sounds is a form of music, too. I want my classroom to be alive with sounds that please the ear and gladden the heart. I want music to be a part of each day at school and of each hour of that day.

The most important thing about music is that it should be ever present in the classroom.

Some important questions to ask yourself are:

1. Have you thought about the different kinds of music you might use in your classroom?
2. If you think you have little musical talent, how will you compensate for this in order to have music in your classroom?
3. Do you play an instrument to accompany your singing?
4. To what extent will you depend on records and tapes for classroom music?
5. How will you respond to a child who doesn't want to sing? What options do you have?
6. Have you surveyed your parents to find out which ones may be able to contribute to your music program?
7. Will you ask children to share favorite songs they have learned at home?

FROM MONARCHS TO MAPLE SYRUP: SCIENCE FOR ALL SEASONS

For some years I have offered a science workshop for preschool teachers called "From Monarchs to Maple Syrup: Preschool Science for All Seasons." The first time I did it, I wasn't really sure that I had much to offer. But by the end of the first session, I felt I had turned a corner. What went on among the 22 teachers and myself as we shared information and experiences was totally exhilarating. My role was more of a facilitator than a teacher; but when we completed our first session, it was evident that something worthwhile had taken place.

In much the same way as I give my workshop, I set up my classroom with interesting living things for children to learn about and care for. Just having living things in the classroom is the first step; wonderful experiences are bound to follow. Just by watching an animal on a daily basis, children learn how it moves, eats, and sleeps. They are learning how to observe carefully — the first step in being a scientist.

I start collecting my classroom menagerie in earnest toward the end of August. It takes time and concentrated effort, but it is all worthwhile when I see what follows. By the opening of school in mid-September, I hope to have on hand one very gentle guinea pig, one or two toads, one or two frogs, a dozen or more red efts, and as many Monarch and Swallowtail caterpillars and butterflies as I can find. This is really more than enough to start with.

I would prefer to introduce one species at a time over the winter months, but Mother Nature has a different plan. The frogs and toads will dig into the earth to hibernate. The red efts will hide in the woods. The Monarch caterpillars will turn into butterflies and will want to head south to Mexico. The Swallowtail caterpillars may overwinter in their chrysalids, but the Swallowtail butterflies will die.

Our guinea pig, "Little Nose," has her own metal cage, which the children help to refurbish each day with fresh water, fresh pellets, and fresh greens. Her house is an inverted shoe box with a cut-out door. The children tear newspapers into strips to make a cozy bedding. On the wall above the cage is a chart that lists the names of the children who will take her home each weekend. Being able to see their name on the list heightens the children's anticipation of the weekend visit.

The frogs and toads live together in a rectangular glass terrarium covered with a fitted screen. A long plastic box with a rock in it makes an ideal pond. And by adding dirt, moss, ground pine, and pine needles, we create a miniature woods. The red efts have a similar environment, but without the pond, in a 10-inch bowl the top of which is covered with Saran Wrap.

When the Monarch caterpillars are small they live in a plastic breadbox, the bottom of which is covered with a moist paper towel. We keep the milkweed leaves they eat fresh by putting the stems in a small glass vial filled with water. At night we cover the breadbox with netting secured by a large rubberband. Later, as the caterpillars grow larger, we transfer them to an institutional-sized mayonnaise jar, which has a small branch in it mounted in plasticene. The jar is set into a butterfly cage made of a crate painted pastel yellow and covered with netting the same color. The Swallowtail chrysalids are attached to the inside of a pint Mason jar.

Obtaining food for all these creatures adds to the fascination of having them in the classroom. Both the children and I bring in treats for the guinea pig to supplement the dry pellets the school buys in bulk. A guinea pig will not eat anything that is harmful to it, so we can experiment to our heart's content. When we make vegetable soup, "Little Nose" has a party. We give her carrot tops and green beans and pea pods galore. Over the years, we have discovered that she even likes tomatoes and pears. In the spring she relishes being taken outside in the sunshine. We place her on the ground inside a tire, where she can nibble the grass and weeds. Toads and frogs are big on spiders and worms — actually, almost any small insect, as long as it is alive.

In addition to our classroom creatures, when weather permits in the fall and spring, we take to the woods to see what we can find. There, we roll over dead logs, lift rocks, and dig in the earth. One day in our exploring we found a spotted salamander.

One of the children's favorite activities is going on a worm hunt on the parking lot after a heavy rain. The children race to pick up the earthworms and put them in paper cups. Caught up in the excitement of the game, even the faint-hearted find the courage to pick up the wiggly worms. Needless to say, the toads and frogs have a heyday. I also buy mealworms for the toads and frogs to supplement their diet. Mealworms must also be fed, but this is easy to do with bran, oatmeal, or common grains found in most kitchen cupboards. The mealworm is the larval stage of a beetle; so to delay the metamorphosis, I refrigerate them and make certain the container is covered with netting secured with a rubber band. The red efts seem to survive on just vegetation, but we give them a treat occasionally by putting ants into their woodsy environment.

Come January, when the frogs and toads are hibernating, I bring in two chameleons. Their favorite food is crickets, which I purchase at the pet shop. We keep the crickets in a small plastic fish bowl with sand for bedding. For water we put a piece of moistened cotton in their bowl each day. They will eat bits of cracker, pretzels, or almost anything. I have found that half a small new potato or slice of apple is to their liking, and it makes cricket housekeeping easier.

"Cloudy," a Dutch Belted rabbit, was a classroom resident for two years. The children and I loved to watch her roam around the school, hopping from one classroom to another. However, finding a home for her at school vacation time, coupled with her less than endearing personal habits, led us to donate her to the Stamford Nature Center. I have heard good reports about other school rabbits. Unfortunately, "Cloudy" was not an exemplary one. Over the years other classroom residents have included a hermit crab and a dozen snails; but neither generated much interest from the children, so they were not repeat residents.

Each year we also have animal visitors from the children's or the teachers' homes. So far this year we have had four visitors: "Caramel," a lopped-eared rabbit; "Puff Ball," a tiny tan mouse; "Precious," my co-worker's golden retriever; and "Applesauce," my daughter's yellow labrador. "Precious" and "Applesauce" are oldtimers, both in age and in coming to nursery school. Both are 11 years old and seem to enjoy the children as much as the children enjoy them. The children paint pictures of them and name

Spirits are high as the children wave goodbye to the Monarch butterflies and wish them a safe journey to Mexico.

their stuffed animals after them. "Precious" and "Applesauce" have become a part of their lives.

Science for preschoolers includes much more than having animals to observe and care for in the classroom. It covers a multitude of things. Cooking is science, and we cook each week. Working with magnets is science. Working with batteries, wires, and bulbs to make lighthouses is science. Planting peas, radishes, and marigolds is science, too. Putting appleseeds in moistened cotton and then in a plastic bag to refrigerate for three months (to simulate the winter) is science. Doing sink-and-float experiments and making ice in the freezer and in the out-of-doors is science. With all of these activities and many more, we talk about and think about why things happen, and we do experiments to make things happen.

In the spring we tap our maple tree and cook down the sap right in our classroom. As we watch it cook down, the delicious aroma permeates the classroom. Then we eat the sweet syrup on either French toast or pancakes we have made.

In the spring we spend a lot of time in the woods and along a small stream, which is just 20 feet from our playground. We look for quartz rocks, sprouting acorns, and whatever other treasures we can unearth. The children use their hands or sticks to remove old leaves, rocks, and mud to create a rushing waterfall. Last week, as we worked away, two red-tailed hawks circled in the sky above us.

I want to provide young children the opportunity to observe, to smell, to taste, to feel, to hear all kinds of things. I want them to observe change and to find out why those changes take place. I want children to be interested in the world around them and to be part of that world as much as possible. I want them to be involved with Monarchs and maple syrup. I want them to experience science for all seasons.

The most important thing about preschool science is that children have the opportunity for hands-on investigation of the world around them.

Some important questions to ask yourself are:

1. How will you go about setting up a science area in your classroom?
2. Are you aware of the science concepts that can be learned by having animals in your classroom?
3. What animals are you comfortable handling?
4. Are you prepared to undertake the on-going care required for keeping an animal in the classroom?
5. When doing a cooking project, will you allow time for the children to taste and smell the ingredients?
6. Will you pre-test a new recipe at home before trying it out in the classroom?
7. Have you considered setting up a "smelling" game in which the children guess what a substance is by smelling it before they actually see it?
8. Do you mind getting your hands dirty while digging with the children out in the woods?
9. What can you do to make scientific attitudes permeate the atmosphere of your classroom?

A BOOK IS A SPECIAL KIND
OF FRIEND

I like being around books. I like the way they look. I like the way they feel. I like the thoughts they convey. When my first child, Jane, was born, I started collecting children's books in earnest. I wanted her to grow up loving books and loving their beautiful illustrations. Both words and illustrations convey messages in their own way. Finding books that are excellent on both counts takes some searching. So much is in the eye of the beholder. So much is a matter of personal taste.

As a teacher, I feel the same way I did as a parent. I want the children in the classroom to experience the richness of a good book. I want them to hear those same stories and see those same illustrations. I want them to grow up loving books and loving beautiful illustrations. There is a timeless quality to an excellent book.

We have story time almost every day, right after our quiet time. This year I made a small change in how I read a story. I no longer sit on a chair in front of the class. Instead, I put myself on the children's level by sitting on one of their rest mats. It seems to make the reading and listening experience a more intimate exchange.

I often read a book to an individual child or a small group — usually by request. Sometimes when a child is feeling sad, there is nothing quite as comforting as listening to a story on the teacher's lap. It never ceases to amaze me how, when I start to read to a single child or a small group, others nearby gather around to listen in. Books create a special world for young children. Books give their imaginations wings with which to fly. Books can lift their spirits and soothe their souls. A book is a special kind of friend.

Below is a list of of book titles that are some of my personal favorites. Some were published more than 50 years ago, but they continue to appeal to young children. They are listed chronologically by year of publication.

Flack, Marjorie. *Ask Mr. Bear*. New York: Collier Books, 1932.

Leaf, Munro. *Ferdinand*. New York: Viking Press, 1936.

Slobodkina, Esphyr. *Caps for Sale*. Reading, Mass.: Scott Young Books, 1940.

McCloskey, Robert. *Make Way for Ducklings*. New York: Viking, 1941.

Brown, Wise M. *The Runaway Bunny*. New York: Harper & Row, 1942.

Brown, Wise M. *Little Chickens*. New York: Harper & Row, 1943.

Weisgard, Leonard. *Whose Little Bird Am I?* New York: Thomas Crowell, 1944.

Brown, Wise M. *Little Fur Family*. New York: Harper & Row, 1946.

Brown, Wise M. *Goodnight Moon*. New York: Harper & Row, 1947.

Krauss, Ruth. *The Growing Story*. New York: Harper & Row, 1947.

Brown, Wise M. *Wait Till the Moon Is Full*. New York: Harper & Row, 1948.

Brown, Wisc M. *The Important Book*. New York: Harper & Row, 1949.

Brown, Wise M. *Fox Eyes*. New York: Pantheon Books, 1951.

Krauss, Ruth. *The Bundle Book*. New York: Harper and Brothers, 1951.

Yashima, Taro. *Crow Boy*. New York: Viking, 1955.

Zion, Gene. *Harry the Dirty Dog*. New York: Harper & Row, 1956.

Minarik, Else Holmelund. *Little Bear*. New York: Harper and Brothers, 1957.

Zion, Gene. *No Roses for Harry*. New York: Harper & Row, 1958.

Lionni, Leo. *Little Blue and Little Yellow*. New York: Ivan Obolensky, 1959.

Lionni, Leo. *Inch By Inch*. New York: Ivan Obolensky, 1960.

Minarik, Else Holmelund. *Little Bear's Visit*. New York: Harper & Row, 1961.

Keats, Ezra Jack. *Snowy Day*. New York: Viking, 1962.

Zolotow, Charlotte. *Mr. Rabbit and the Lovely Present*. New York: Harper & Row, 1962.

Hoban, Russell. *Bread and Jam for Frances*. New York: Harper & Row, 1964.

Keats, Ezra Jack. *Jennie's Hat*. New York: Harper & Row, 1966.

Keats, Ezra Jack. *Peter's Chair*. New York: Harper & Row, 1967.

Freeman, Don. *Corduroy*. New York: Viking, 1968.

Sitting on the children's level makes the reading and listening a more intimate experience.

Lionni, Leo. *Swimmy*. New York: Pantheon, 1968.

Reiss, Steck M. *Thackeray Turtle*. Austin, Texas: Vaughn, 1969.

Lobel, Arnold. *Frog and Toad Are Friends*. New York: Harper & Row, 1970.

Mayers, Patrick. *Just One More Block*. Chicago: Whitman, 1970.

Lobel, Arnold. *Frog and Toad Together*. New York: Harper & Row, 1971.

Arkin, Alan. *Tony's Hard Work Day*. New York: Harper & Row, 1972.

Waber, Bernard. *Ira Sleeps Over*. Boston: Houghton Mifflin, 1972.

Birnbaum, A. *Green Eyes*. Racine, Wisc.: Western, 1973.

Burningham, John. *Mr. Gumpy's Motor Car*. New York: Thomas Crowell, 1973.

Mosel, Arlene. *Tiki Tiki Tembo*. New York: Holt, Rinehart and Winston, 1975.

Leonni, Leo. *Frederick*. New York: Pantheon, 1976.

Ets, Marie Hall. *Gilberto and the Wind*. New York: Viking, 1978.

Whitman, Sally. *A Special Trade*. New York: Harper & Row, 1978.

Frost, Robert. *Stopping by Woods on a Snowy Evening*. New York: E. P. Dutton, 1978.

Hall, Donald. *Ox Cart Man*. New York: Viking, 1979.

Asch, Frank. *Happy Birthday Moon*. Englewood Cliffs, N.J.: Prentice-Hall, 1982.

Thaler, Mike. *Owly*. New York: Harper & Row, 1982.

Carle, Eric. *The Very Hungry Caterpillar*. Cleveland: World, 1984.

Carle, Eric. *The Very Busy Spider*. Cleveland: World, 1984.

Locker, Thomas. *Where the River Begins*. New York: Dial Books, 1984.

Wildsmith, Brian. *The Owl and the Woodpecker*. New York: Oxford University Press, 1984.

Day, Alexandra. *Good Dog, Carl*. La Jolla, Calif.: Green Tiger Press, 1985.

Locker, Thomas. *The Mare on the Hill*. New York: Dial Books, 1985.

Yolen, Jane. *Owl Moon*. New York: Putnam, 1987.

The most important thing about a good book is that it touches the child's world and affords new glimpses of a larger world.

Some important questions to ask yourself are:

1. Does your enthusiasm for good children's books come through to the children?
2. Do you plan to teach children how to care for books?
3. Are you prepared to re-read a story many times because the children ask you to?
4. Do you encourage children to bring in their favorite book from home to share with the class?
5. Are your prepared to reject reading a book a child has brought from home because you find it inappropriate for the age group?
6. Do you on occasion check out a selection of books from the local library to supplement the ones available in the classroom?
7. Do you call attention to the illustrations as you read the text?
8. Have you considered letting children dictate a story to you so they can "write" their own book?

ART IS FOR EVERYDAY

When my three children were young, I was fortunate in being able to be at home with them. My primary work then was caring for my young family. I remember writing to an old friend and telling her that what I was doing was creating a beautiful environment for my family. Now those children are adults, but I am still creating beautiful environments for young children.

There is little in life that remains the same. We accommodate and we adjust. But, for me, the quest for beauty never changes. Wherever I am, be it tramping the woods on Stuart Island in New Zealand, walking on Charing Cross Road in London, or looking around my classroom in White Plains, New York, my eye seeks out what is beautiful. When that happens, I find my hands work to please the eye.

I want the children in nursery school to live each school day within a beautiful environment — an environment that is not only seen but one that is deeply felt. Art projects we do each day are part of this environment. The products adorn our walls and our windows; they stand on window ledges, hang on the drying rack, or wait in cubbies to be taken home. On-going art projects contribute much to the beautiful environment of our classroom. But there is more to art projects than just the products.

I did my first master's thesis on art in a kindergarten classroom. Through daily anecdotal records and photographs, I chronicled a child's emotional development through his artistic endeavors. These endeavors could be paintings, they could be blocks, they could be dictated stories. Any medium can be a vehicle to foster growth. It is what one does with the medium, how one feels while working with the medium, and how others react to what one has created that stimulates growth. Involving children in a variety of interesting art projects gives them a sense of accomplishment when they see what they have created with their own hands. And when the teacher praises their efforts, children's self-esteem increases.

Through the years I have kept a log of all the art projects I have used with children. Some of them I have borrowed from other teachers in my school; some I learned about by visiting other schools; some have come from parents who volunteered to conduct an art project in my class. Some of these projects have been more successful than others; but from the variety I have tried, I have come up with some principles that guide the art activities in my classroom.

First, I use only materials that are aesthetically pleasing to me. Nursery school teachers (myself included) are inveterate collectors of things — always with the thought that they can make use of them sometime. I find it difficult to throw things out, but I force myself to do so if I think the materials are not aesthetically pleasing. Second, I firmly believe in the value of repetition. Often I will set out the same art project materials for two consecutive days. This allows a child to see the product of work done the day before, which may spark his imagination to use the same materials for a quite different project. Repetition is experimentation. Repetition is practice. Both are worthwhile for a young child.

A third principle is to work from the simple to the complex. When selecting a project at the beginning of the year, keep it simple. As the year progresses and children develop greater dexterity in handling tools and materials, they can take on more complex projects and grace old materials with new ideas. Repetition becomes a new experience.

When the children return to school after a long holiday, spirits are spilling over. We haven't seen each other for many days; there is so much to talk about. I find playdough to be a calming medium. It feels good; it is easy to manipulate. It is a material that a child can work with and still carry on a conversation with a classmate or the teacher. It provides a child a calming and satisfying re-entry into the world of school.

I have strong feelings about the size and quality of paper children use for their painting. For young children I like painting paper that measures 24-by-18 inches. Young children need a large space to paint on, just as they need a lot of space to run and jump. It gives them a freedom of movement. I also like to use a thick, very white paper called white sulphite. It provides a bright contrasting background for the children's paintings.

I generally have eight chairs at the art tables. If we are using extra-large paper, I set up places for only four painters. Sometimes I will take away the chairs and have the children paint standing up to give them a different perspective. Or I will put the paper in a vertical rather than a horizontal position, also to give them a different perspective. Sometimes I will put the two tables end to end when we are working on a large group mural. I cover the tables with several layers of newspaper. It makes cleanup easy when I can whisk off the paint-spattered top layer of newspaper and have a clean surface for the next child to paint on.

For collage work we generally use Elmer's glue, which we buy by the gallon. We keep the glue in four clear plastic pill containers with white screw tops and use craft sticks to apply the glue. For paper collage work we sometimes use library paste, which the children can apply with their fingers. We purchase water soluble, non-toxic paint by the gallon. Because dried paint tends to make the covers of the paint containers stick, I put vaseline around the threads at the top. It saves us a lot of frustration.

At the beginning of the school year, the children have their first art experience painting at the easels with two colors. We use six-ounce juice cans to hold the paint. They are plentiful and can be disposed of, but they can be easily cleaned and reused. I keep a bottle brush at the sink for cleaning the cans. Soaking helps. As the year progresses, I gradually add more colors to give the children more choice in their paintings. At some point I will add white to each color to make pastels to add to the repertoire of colors available.

In the spring I introduce palettes for mixing colors. The palettes are made of 11-by-11-inch pieces of composition board. I show children who are interested how to mix colors together on the pallette and then use the new colors for their paintings. Many children find it fascinating just to mix the paints to make new colors. I also have a three-inch roll of clear cellophane, which I cut into strips for the children to press onto their wet paintings. It adds a shiny layer to their paintings that delights the artist and the beholder.

Following is a list of art projects I have used successfully with young children.

Collage

1. Shells and sand. Done on cardboard covered with pale blue paper.

2. Leaves, bittersweet, pine cones, pine needles, sweet gum pods, and bark. Done on cardboard covered with tan burlap.

3. Fall leaves. Done on white cardboard with Elmer's glue thinned with water. Glue can be put on both the underneath and the top surface of the leaves.

4. Different textures — leather, fur, velvet, etc., glued to cardboard.

5. Cardboard tubes of varying sizes glued on cardboard. These can be painted the next day.

6. Sawdust and wood pieces glued on a wooden base.

7. Box collage on inverted box lids. These can be painted on the second day.

8. Various shapes and colors of corrugated paper. Done on cardboard.

9. Small pieces of styrofoam glued to a large styrofoam base.

10. Different shapes and colors of styrofoam glued to cardboard or heavy paper.

11. Different lengths and colors of thin yarn glued onto white cardboard.

12. One-color collage, for example, green cellophane, green construction paper, green ribbon, and green yarn. Done on white cardboard.

13. Precut strips of different colored construction paper. Pasted onto cardboard covered with construction paper. Library paste can be used.

14. Craft sticks colored with magic markers. Glued to cardboard or heavy paper.

15. Painted toilet tissue rolls cut into various sizes. Done on cardboard.

16. Different shapes and colors of cellophane. Pasted on waxed paper.

17. Pieces of colored tissue paper on waxed paper using liquid starch as the adhesive. (This gives the appearance of a stained glass window when taped on the windows.)

18. Different shapes and colors of construction paper. Children cut their own shapes and paste them on a contrasting color of construction paper.

19. Pieces of fabric. Done on cardboard.

Lynne's art project today was making a birthday crown for her stuffed animal.

Painting

1. Eye-dropper painting with two colors on construction paper.

2. Q-tip painting with two colors on construction paper.

3. Sponge painting, using small pieces of sponges, with two colors on construction paper.

4. Tempera magic dot painting in a variety of colors on construction paper.

5. A combination of thin strands of yarn and paint on white cardboard.

6. Straw blowing of paint on construction paper. The paint should be thinned with water and placed on the paper with an

eye-dropper. The air blown through the straw distributes the paint in interesting patterns.

7. Painting with foam rubber brushes.

8. Painting on cardboard covered with aluminum foil.

9. String painting with two colors.

10. Painting cardboard egg cartons. A big favorite with young children.

11. Painting "cookies" made of playdough. Glazing with Elmer's glue once the paint is dried.

12. Painting on textured wallpaper.

13. Painting with white paint on black construction paper.

14. Self-portraits. A child lies down on a long piece of brown craft paper, and the teacher traces around the child's body with a crayon or magic marker. The child then paints the outline in colors he chooses.

15. Finger painting on formica-top tables. Warning: limit of two children per table.

Printing

1. Print of a finger painting. A sheet of white paper is placed over the wet finger painting and smoothed down. Then lift off the paper to show the print. This is best done by the teacher.

2. Printing with hornets' nests, acorns, sweet gum pods, other textured items found in nature. Done on construction paper.

3. Printing with the rims of paper cups on construction paper. Use two colors of paint and two or three different size cups.

4. Using a thick pencil, impress a design on a large block of styrofoam. Then paint and print.

Rubbings

1. Tape thin paper to textured vinyl floor tiles. Rub with the side of an unwrapped crayon.

2. Put thin paper over different textured materials such as nylon netting or the side of a plastic berry box. Rub with the side of an unwrapped crayon.

3. Place leaves under thin paper and rub with the side of an unwrapped crayon.

Dyeing

1. Fold a paper towel into a fan and dip in water with a strong solution of food coloring. Press dry between newspaper.

2. Use eye-droppers and strong food coloring to make a colored pattern on white paper towels.

3. Fold white tissue paper and dip the corners into food coloring.

4. Dye strips of white sheets with food coloring.

5. Tie dye white T-shirts using clothing dye and rubberbands. Each child brings a T-shirt from home.

Miscellaneous

1. Drawing with large pieces of chalk on wet construction paper.

2. Using pastels on paper.

3. Sculpting with clay, using only the hands as the modeling tool.

4. Building shapes with wet sand.

5. Folding and cutting colored construction paper.

6. Cornstarch painting with cardboard "combs." Cornstarch recipe: Mix eight tablespoons of cornstarch with eight tablespoons of water. Add one quart of boiling water and bring to a boil. Cool and add liquid food coloring.

7. Line inside of a large box lid with finger paint paper. Use four marbles and food coloring or thinned tempera paint and make patterns by rolling the marbles around the box lid.

8. Shrink-a-dinks. Made with 4-by-8-inch ribbed clear plastic meat trays colored with permanent magic markers. Bake at 250 degrees on middle shelf of a toaster oven for about five minutes. Watch carefully to avoid melting. Before baking, make hole with hole puncher so shrink-a-dink can be worn as a pendant.

9. Make bird nests with dried grasses, moss, leaves, twigs, pine needles, feathers, and mud. Use a styrofoam meat tray as a base. Gathering the materials for the nests makes this activity a springtime favorite.

10. Make miniature trees by mounting twigs or small branches in plasticene. Cut triangular leaves out of construction paper and punch holes in them so they can be hung on the tree. This project can be done twice, once in the fall using red, orange, and yellow "leaves," and again in the spring using all shades of green "leaves."

11. Tissue paper flowers with pipe cleaner stems.

12. Giant caterpillars made from the inverted bottom half of a cardboard egg carton. After painting in bright colors, two pipe cleaners are inserted as antennae.

13. Binoculars made from two painted toilet tissue rolls stapled together. Punch two holes for attaching a strap to go around the neck. This activity is timed to coincide with fall and spring bird walks.

14. Kaleidoscope made with a paper towel roll into which a toilet tissue roll is inserted. Paint both rolls the first day. Put sequins, small ribbon pieces, colored gravel, and crayon shavings between two sheets of cellophane and secure with a rubber band on one end of the roll.

15. Kite made in the shape of a butterfly. The wings measuring about 18 inches are made of thick paper. They can be decorated with gummed circles and squares, and a 12-inch strip of a colorful fabric is stapled to the body as a tail. Punch holes between the wings and reinforce with gummed circles. Tie a six-foot string through the holes and attach the other end to a craft stick. As the children run, the kite flies in back of them. A very successful spring project.

16. Flags made with the thin cardboard tube found on wire coat hangers. The flag, made of construction paper decorated with magic markers, is taped to the tube.

17. Paper bag masks with cut-outs for eyes, nose, and shoulders. Paint masks on the first day. Decorate with yarn, buttons, pieces of fabric, etc., on the second day.

18. Necklace made with a piece of yarn onto which is threaded cut up pieces of striped plastic straws and small pieces of construction paper punched with a hole. Threading is easier if the ends of the yarn are bound with a piece of tape.

19. Mobiles made from wire coat hangers bent into interesting forms. Buttons, feathers, straws, beads, and other objects attached to wire, string, or "Twistems" hang from the mobile.

20. Buildings made with different size cream and milk cartons, which have been painted and taped together. Cut-out doors and windows made of construction paper can be added the second day. The buildings can be taped on a cardboard base for those who want to add gardens and trees. These buildings are often used in conjunction with block construction.

21. Group mural made on brown craft paper and three-inch painted cardboard squares. The first day the colored squares are glued on the paper. The second day a one-color background is painted on the paper.

22. Group patchwork quilt made with sheets of different colored paper taped together on the underneath side. Added decoration is possible by cutting out different colored shapes of construction paper and gluing them on top.

I want the children's eyes to seek out what is beautiful. I want the children to use their hands to please their eyes. I want art to be part of their every day. The most important thing to remember about art projects in nursery school is that children should have opportunities every day to create artistically pleasing objects.

Some important questions to ask yourself are:

1. Are you selective about the materials you provide children for their art projects? Are they pleasing to you? Are they safe to use? OSHA, the Occupational Safety and Health Administration, publishes periodical reports on the safety of art materials. The address is: Room 3445, 1515 Broadway, New York, NY 10036. Phone: (212) 944-3423.

2. Are you familiar with commercial sources of quality art materials?

3. Do you plan art projects far enough ahead so that you have the necessary materials on hand?

4. Have you considered inviting a parent to direct an art project with your class?

5. Do you talk to other teachers about their successful art projects?

6. Do you visit art exhibitions or attend art seminars to stimulate your own thinking?

7. Have you considered inviting an art specialist to conduct a hands-on art workshop for the staff?

8. Do you take the time to sit beside children to watch them work and listen to what they say about their projects?

9. Do you offer encouragement and praise for a child's art work?

THE COGNITIVE CLAMOR

Each year parents come to our school to see if it is the kind of a nursery school they want for their child. I try to get a reading on them from what they do and say. I watch the expressions on their faces. I notice if they insist on standing up, or if they sit down and put themselves on the children's level. Mostly, I just listen to their questions.

Most parents ask me about the typical schedule for the morning and if we spend time outdoors each day. These are certainly appropriate questions. Some parents talk about the specific needs of their child, particularly if the child is currently in a school where things are not going well. Some are interested in how much music we have. Some ask me how much reading readiness I do in the classroom. If this is the only question they ask, it gives me pause.

My daughter, Jane, is in the process of selecting a nursery school for her son, Lawrence Pierre. Because she has visited my classroom countless times and is by nature a keen observer, we can talk in considerable depth about the nature of four-year-olds and the kind of learning environment they need. Just this week she visited a prestigious laboratory nursery school in Massachusetts, which had a computer in the classroom. Jane asked some very direct questions. The mere presence of a computer at the nursery school level says much about the cognitive clamor.

At our school the main thrust is to help children to grow and understand themselves, their peers, and the adults around them. Our method of helping children understand the world around them is to involve them in all kinds of hands-on experiences. Cognitive skills are very definitely a part of each of those experiences. But we have no workbooks. We have no worksheets. The alphabet is not displayed in the classroom. Actually, only a few words are visible. Each child's name is there, on the cubby, on the juice and cracker chart, and on the guinea pig chart showing who will take her home for the weekend. Signs for block buildings are made on request. We do put out a "HOT" sign when we are cooking something that is hot. Generally I use pictures to convey ideas, particularly in the early months of school.

By spring we become more word-oriented. By then the children can recognize their own names and the names of their classmates. Four- and five-year-olds are great rhymers, and they love to do it. I write a three- or four-letter word — cat, dog, red, blue. Then I do a singing game giving each child who wishes a chance to chime in with a rhyme. I leave those words on the blackboard. Once used they tend to stay with us, just like the blocks and the paints and the pictures on the wall. During the year there are other words that go up on the blackboard. The word "juice" is there, followed by a list of children's names who want to prepare our frozen, concentrated orange juice. I don't point out the individual letters of the word "juice." There is no flash card with the word "juice" on it. But the children know that it is the word they look at when they want to know whose turn it is to prepare the juice.

We do a lot of counting each day. When we do our cleanup of the block area, I ask one child to give us a "magic" number. If it is "seven," then we carry seven blocks at a time and put them back on the block shelf. They count the crackers or the pretzels for snack time. They count the number of crickets that are given to the chameleons. They count the number of mealworms that are given to the toads. They count the number of pockets they have on their pants. They count the number of barrettes Cathy has in her hair. We have only one visible number in the classroom (number 1), which goes from cubby to cubby to show who is first in line for cleanup time. Otherwise there are no numbers displayed around the room.

I read articles in the newspaper about youngsters who are going to special schools to cram their minds with words and numbers. "Hothouse Tots," the headline calls them. Hothousing for what? To get into a better prep school? To get into a better college? To lead a better life? It makes me sad to think what these children and their parents are missing.

Yesterday I spoke with my grandson, Lawrence, on the telephone. He told me that he still had a few chocolate Easter eggs

These young "scientists" are learning to be careful observers as they watch the movements of the small red efts.

left. There was a long pause. Then, in his small voice, he said, "You know I tried to stay awake so I could see the Easter Bunny." I told Lawrence that I also stayed up hoping to see the Easter Bunny, but like him, I, too, had fallen fast asleep. There is so much to enjoy in the child's world. There are so few years for a child to be a child. The presence of too many letters, too many words, too many numbers, or a computer can dull the imagination and put unnecessary pressure on this precious time of life.

The most important thing to remember about the cognitive clamor is to keep it in perspective. Young children can and do learn all kinds of cognitive skills in a natural and unpressured classroom environment.

Some important questions to ask yourself are:

1. How will you respond to the parent who asks you what you are doing about reading readiness?
2. What activites in your classroom can you use to give children experience with counting and number concepts.

3. Do you believe that showing your enthusiasm for a book you read during storytime might be more important than teaching the alphabet?
4. Is fostering young children's love of books perhaps more important than learning to read?
5. Do you play many rhyming games with the children? Do you praise them for being good poets?
6. Do you let the children choose a favorite picture and dictate a story to you about it?

BUILDING TRUST

As an adult in the classroom I have many roles to fill. I want to be positive, supportive, enthusiastic, curious, patient, interested, calm, fair, experimental, humorous, and sometimes even a bit poetic. I want to be all these things and be good at each of them. But as I think about all these positive qualities, I have come to believe that the most important quality of all is being authentic. More than anything else I want to be believable. I want to be real. I want to be an adult in whom children have trust.

Trust comes through a building process. It is being there at the door each morning with a warm welcome. It is making the room and playground a safe place for a child to be. It is setting limits on behavior in the classroom and playground with rules that are clearly defined and clearly understood. It is being at a child's level so that I can listen better. It is remembering what a child says, remembering my response, and then doing what I said I would do. It is being consistent in my thoughts and actions so the children know what to expect. It is encouraging a child to do more with blocks than just stacking one on top of another and then being there to praise him when he makes a helicopter with a door later in the day. It is finding a caterpillar on the playground and calling the children together to look up its name in our caterpillar book and find out what it likes to eat. It is giving Nathan all the time he needs to tell the group what he's going to wear for Halloween. It is giving Rachel all the time she needs to tie her shoe laces.

Trust comes through a building process. For me, it means keeping lots of lists so that everyone gets a turn — a turn to make the orange juice and deliver it to the other classrooms, a turn to turn out the lights before rest time, a turn to take the guinea pig home for the weekend, or a turn to deliver the rolled-up paintings to each child's cubby on Friday by matching the name on the paintings to the name on the cubbies. It means writing a reminder on the blackboard that Carl wanted to start a painting just as work time ended on Tuesday and should have an easel first thing on Wednesday morning. It means using our three-minute timer so that if John wants to wear the red hard hat or Karen wants to wear the "gold" necklace, they don't have to wait too long. It means being fair — day in and day out throughout the whole year.

Trust comes through a building process. It is treating each child as though he counts. It is telling Jennifer that the note she is taking home talks about the Book Fair that will be held in school next week. It is reading to David the note that his mommy sent that says he wants to visit Scott in another classroom but isn't sure how to do it. It is telling Tim that his daddy just called on the telephone to say that Tim cried when the carpool came this morning and didn't really want to come to school. It is showing the whole class the parent conference sign-up sheet posted on our blue classroom door and explaining to them what it is all about. It is telling the children that they are invited, too, if their mommies and daddies want them to be there. It is showing them their mommies' and daddies' names, addresses, and phone numbers posted on our bulletin board. It is showing the children a special file in the front office with a card for each of them, which tells us how to reach daddy at the office, their pediatrician, or a special friend of the family in case of an emergency. It is sharing with a child what is going on in his world.

Trust comes through a building process. It is showing children that you can learn from them as well. This year it is giving the teacher a turn at turning out the lights at rest time, because it was David's idea. It is calling the juice pitchers measuring cups, because Jamie says that is what they really are. It is respecting children for their ideas and suggestions.

Trust comes through a building process. It is showing a child that you can make mistakes, too — that you can make a terrible mess when shaking up a gallon of blue paint and the top comes off and the paint goes all over your blue jeans and on the floor. They understand when you say you could use some help in cleaning it up. Sarah needs to know that the teacher can sometimes forget to read a storybook that she brought to school. Paul needs to know that sometimes you can't remember all the words to "Clap Your Hands, Touch Your Toes." Mary needs to know that the pumpkin bread didn't taste so great because the teacher took it out of the oven too soon. Children need to know that sometimes a teacher loses track of time and there isn't enough time to finish cleanup before they have to go to creative movement class in another room. They need to know that sometimes a teacher can say, "I have a sore throat today, so I'm going to try to have a quiet morning." They need to know that sometimes the teacher can say, "I am angry when you push Jake off the ladder." Children need to know that you, like they, are less than perfect.

Children also need to know that you can clean up that spilled blue paint and read that special story the next day, that you can practice the words to "Clap Your Hands, Touch Your Toes," and that they can make pumpkin bread again that will taste great. The class needs to know that next Friday we'll try to be on time when Mrs. Bates comes to collect everyone for creative movement class. The class needs to know that a sore throat goes away and that the teacher doesn't stay angry.

As a teacher, I want to be authentic. More than anything else I want to be believable. I want to be real; I want to be an adult in whom children have trust. The most important thing to remember is that by being authentic, by being yourself, you will earn the trust of young children.

Some important questions to ask yourself are:

1. Is fostering trust one of your primary goals for the year?
2. As a teacher, do you feel that you must have answers to everything that comes up?
3. How do you show that you are open to learning from children?
4. When you make a mistake, are you willing to admit it to the class?
5. Can you laugh at yourself?
6. Have you devised a system so that all children have equal opportunities to participate in activities?
7. How do you show children that you are consistent in thought and action and follow through on what you say you will do?
8. What kinds of age-appropriate information will you share with your class?
9. Have you set new goals for yourself regarding being authentic and building trust?

ENDINGS AND BEGINNINGS

It is a flawless March day at my farm in Massachusetts with the sun shining down out of a cloudless sky. I am walking in my orchard picking up the prunings and setting them into windrows. It seems as if I know personally each tree in the orchard. I have watched each one change from an untamed and uncared for neglected child into a well-groomed and cherished member of the family. Just being in the orchard gives me a tremendous sense of satisfaction and well-being. It is my favorite place on earth.

On that March Sunday in 1985 as I walked among the trees in the orchard, I spotted something blue lying on the ground. I bent down to pick it up and saw that the blue object was a deflated balloon. Despite the dirt on one side, I could see a small white piece of paper rolled up inside the balloon. I removed the tightly rolled scroll and read the following message:

My name is Stanley Janicki. I am a resident of Americana-East, 600 S. Webster Avenue, Green Bay, Wisconsin, 54301. Please write and tell me where you found my balloon.

I took the balloon and the note back to school and told the children about it. Together we decided to write a letter to Mr. Janicki, asking him when he sent the balloon and what he had used to fill it. We told him we wanted to send up our own balloons. In just six days we had our response. This is what the letter said:

I was very excited to receive your letter! It had been so long since we sent the balloons that everyone at the nursing home was surprised.

December 10, 1984, was the 20th anniversary of Americana-East and as part of our celebration we launched the balloons. Each of the balloons was filled with helium, a special gas that helps them float in the air.

I have lived at Americana for 2½ years. I am 94 years old. I am retired, but I used to make cheese. I worked in a small town in northern Wisconsin called Thorp. My favorite thing to do is to eat popcorn. I also like to sit outside in the summer, and I play bingo two times a week.

All of us at Americana were excited to read your letter. We told the newspaper and they printed a short story. I am sending that along for you to read.

With warm regards,
Stanley Janicki and the folks at Americana

We all were very touched by Mr. Janicki's letter. As I thought more about the letter, I was struck with the similarities between the world of a four-year-old and a 94-year-old. The next day we made popcorn. We played bingo. We spent time outdoors. We made a big batch of popcorn, enough to fill a huge white plastic container, which the children decorated with brightly colored circles and squares. We mailed it to our new friend in Wisconsin. Of course, we ate lots of popcorn, too.

Now that we knew that the balloons were filled with helium, we started making inquiries as to where to purchase our own balloons and get them filled with helium. Each child could select his favorite color balloon. Inside each balloon was a small strip of paper on which was written the child's first name, the name and address of the school, and a brief message asking the finder to write and tell us where he found the balloon — just like Mr. Janicki had done.

We asked the other classrooms to join us in our new venture. Our director called the local paper, the Gannett newspapers, the *New York Post*, and the *New York Times* to tell them how we came to undertake this project. Our favorite photographer, Claire Yaffa, who provided the photographs for this book, said she would be on hand to photograph the event.

Our launch date was set for April 10, 1985. It was a chilly, windy day with the threat of rain. Because the children were wild with excitement and the press had been alerted, we decided to proceed with our original plan. It was a happening, a memorable event in the lives of our young children. On the signal, Ready! Set! Go! 60 balloons soared skyward. Unfortunately, 18 of them got caught in the branches of a nearby maple tree. But the other 42 were a joyous sight to behold, lifting the spirits of young and old alike.

Since the launching, other meaningful and touching things have happened. Mr. Janicki sent a second newspaper clipping from the *Green Bay Press-Gazette* recounting the event. It also quoted Mr. Janicki as saying, "I feel so good about the letter because I don't have any children of my own." We also received a long letter from Mr. Janicki's niece and guardian, Agnes Zastawniak. She told us that she visits her uncle at least twice a week. She had not known about the balloon launching at the nursing home until her most recent visit. She wrote, "He took me by the arm to show me your letter. They have it up on the bulletin board." She told us that her uncle had a major heart operation two years ago. Last year he had a cancerous tumor removed from his vocal chords. She went on to add, "Nothing keeps him down. He is able to get around on his own and is able to talk, but his voice is a little raspy." She told us that his birthday is April 24th. (My late father's birthday was April 24th.)

Because of the coincidence of the birthdays, I told my 86-year-old mother about Mr. Janicki and suggested that she might want to write him. I urged her to tell him about herself, about my farm and the orchard, which she knows well. Mother had had major heart surgery in January. She sent Mr. Janicki three different kinds of popcorn (regular, cheese, and caramel) in a large tin can decorated with early Americana scenes. In his thank-you note to my mother, he wrote, "The can will be a nice reminder of your thoughtfulness as well as brightening up my room."

The children have just completed a very special book, which will arrive at Americana-East in time for Mr. Janicki's 95th birthday. Each pastel-colored page has a color photograph of a child in the class. Underneath each photograph is a story the child dictated, telling what he or she likes to do best. Lisa said, "I like to go to the beach. I like to build big sand castles. I like the waves to tickle my toes." Alice said, "I want to send him a birthday card. I want that he should know my name." Mr. Janicki has become part of our classroom conversation. He has become part of our lives. In endings there are beginnings.

We have six weeks left of the school term. Final conferences are completed. Summer birthday parties have been scheduled for the month of May. Children and their parents are visiting kindergarten. We will soon be leaving each other. Leaving something you love is not easy. Leaving can be filled with mixed emotions.

Part of preparing for a separation is being able to talk about it — being able to talk things through. When we all returned from spring vacation, we started to talk about leaving, about moving on. A book I like to read to the children for setting the stage for talking about leaving is *Will I Have a Friend?* by Miriam Cohen (Macmillan 1967).

As we come to end of the year, I want the children to know I care deeply about each of them. I want them to know I also will care next year. I want them to know I will still be at the nursery school next year, and that the classroom will be much the same. I want them to know they can come to visit school whenever they wish. I want them to know they are welcome here, next year and the year after that as well. I want them to know that they can call me on the telephone and tell me what they are doing. I want them to know that they can write me a letter, and I will answer it.

I want each child to know that kindergarten is an exciting place, where there will be another teacher who cares for them. I want them to know there will be old friends to be with and new friends to make. I want them to know there will be blocks to build with and paints to paint with and new books to look at and new toys to discover. I want them to know they will be going to school on the big yellow school bus and taking a lunch box as well. I want each child to know that kindergarten is the "big time."

In endings there are beginnings.

About the Author

Carol B. Hillman is currently head teacher for four-year-olds at The Nursery School in White Plains, New York, where she has worked for the past 19 years. A native of Kansas City, she currently resides in Harrison, New York, and in the summer at her farm in New Salem, Massachusetts, where she operates an apple orchard and a manufacturing kitchen, producing solar cooked preserves. She also raises and markets dried flowers.

Hillman is a graduate of Smith College and has two master's degrees from Bank Street College of Education in early childhood education and educational leadership. In addition to her nursery school teaching, she has since 1979 conducted seminars for early childhood teachers on "Science for Young Children," sponsored by the Westchester Association for the Education of Young Children.

About the Photographer

Claire Yaffa, a graduate of Sarah Lawrence College, has had a one-woman show at the Hudson River Museum and has exhibited at many galleries in New York City and Philadelphia. A free-lance photographer and specialist in portraiture of children, she has been actively involved for the past 10 years with the Foundation for Children with Learning Disabilities, where her photography has been featured in its annual journal.

For the past eight years, Yaffa has worked with Dr. Vincent Fontana, director of the New York Foundling Hospital and head of the Mayor's Task Force on Child Abuse, in an effort to draw attention to the problem of child abuse and to the need for rehabilitative programs. Her photography for this project culminated in an exhibition at the International Center of Photography in New York City and a publication titled, *Reaching Out.*

Yaffa's most recent work was a project on the homeless in Westchester County, New York, featuring her photography in exhibits at the Bridge Gallery in White Plains, the White Plains Museum Gallery, and at Sarah Lawrence College.